CAMBRIDGE LIBRARY COLLECTION

Books of enduring scholarly value

History

The books reissued in this series include accounts of historical events and movements by eye-witnesses and contemporaries, as well as landmark studies that assembled significant source materials or developed new historiographical methods. The series includes work in social, political and military history on a wide range of periods and regions, giving modern scholars ready access to influential publications of the past.

Dutch Guiana

William Gifford Palgrave (1826–88) was a renowned traveller and Arabic scholar. After graduating from Trinity College, Cambridge, in 1846 he received a lieutenant's commission in the 8th Bombay Regiment of native infantry, but he converted to Roman Catholicism, and settled in Syria as a missionary in 1855, during which time he travelled across Arabia. After renouncing Catholicism in 1865, he began a career with the British foreign service, working in several positions in the Far East. This volume, first published in 1876, contains Palgrave's account of his visit to Dutch Guiana, now the South American country of Suriname. Arranging his material according to geographic location, Palgrave describes in detail the society and geography of the country, discussing the treatment of former slaves and describing the unique Maroon culture composed of former slaves and indigenous people. This volume provides fascinating information on the society and culture of this uniquely diverse country.

Cambridge University Press has long been a pioneer in the reissuing of out-of-print titles from its own backlist, producing digital reprints of books that are still sought after by scholars and students but could not be reprinted economically using traditional technology. The Cambridge Library Collection extends this activity to a wider range of books which are still of importance to researchers and professionals, either for the source material they contain, or as landmarks in the history of their academic discipline.

Drawing from the world-renowned collections in the Cambridge University Library, and guided by the advice of experts in each subject area, Cambridge University Press is using state-of-the-art scanning machines in its own Printing House to capture the content of each book selected for inclusion. The files are processed to give a consistently clear, crisp image, and the books finished to the high quality standard for which the Press is recognised around the world. The latest print-on-demand technology ensures that the books will remain available indefinitely, and that orders for single or multiple copies can quickly be supplied.

The Cambridge Library Collection will bring back to life books of enduring scholarly value (including out-of-copyright works originally issued by other publishers) across a wide range of disciplines in the humanities and social sciences and in science and technology.

Dutch Guiana

WILLIAM GIFFORD PALGRAVE

CAMBRIDGE UNIVERSITY PRESS

Cambridge, New York, Melbourne, Madrid, Cape Town, Singapore,
São Paolo, Delhi, Dubai, Tokyo, Mexico City

Published in the United States of America by Cambridge University Press, New York

www.cambridge.org
Information on this title: www.cambridge.org/9781108024358

© in this compilation Cambridge University Press 2010

This edition first published 1876
This digitally printed version 2010

ISBN 978-1-108-02435-8 Paperback

DUTCH GUIANA.

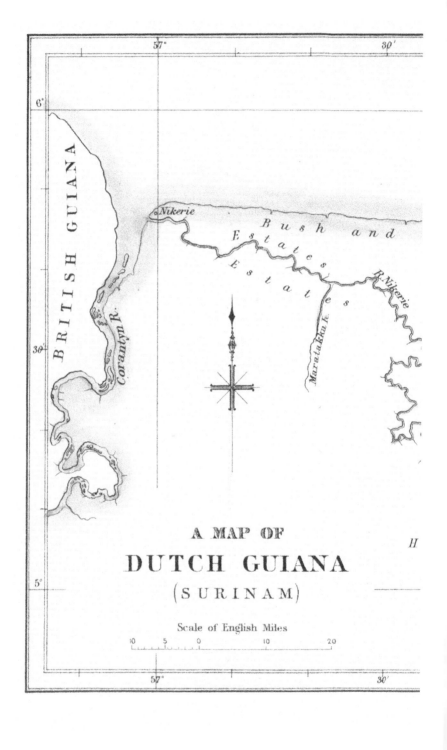

A MAP OF

DUTCH GUIANA

(SURINAM)

Scale of English Miles

A T L A N T I

Bush

Coronie

R. Saramacca

S w a m p   C o t t o n

Batavia

Crom

C o r o n i e

E s t a t e s

W o o d

H i g h   L a n d

R. Coppename

R. Tibitie

R. Coesowine

a n d

a n d   W o o d s

S a v a n n

H i g h   L a n d

i g h   L a n d

B U S H   N E G R O E S

S a v a n n a   a n d   F o r e s t

London: Macmillan & Co.

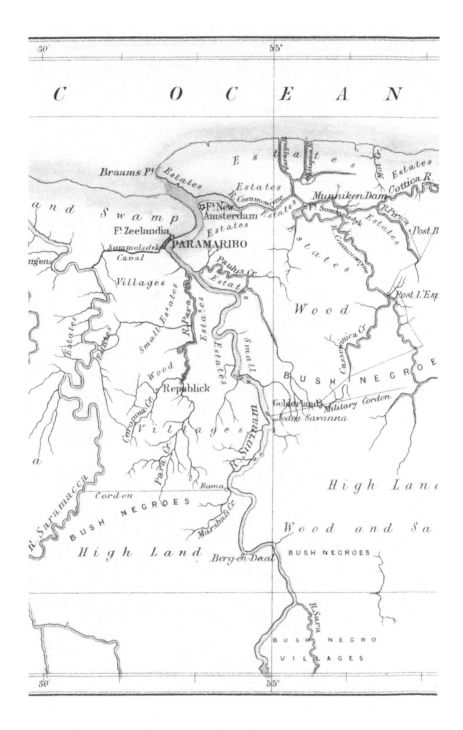

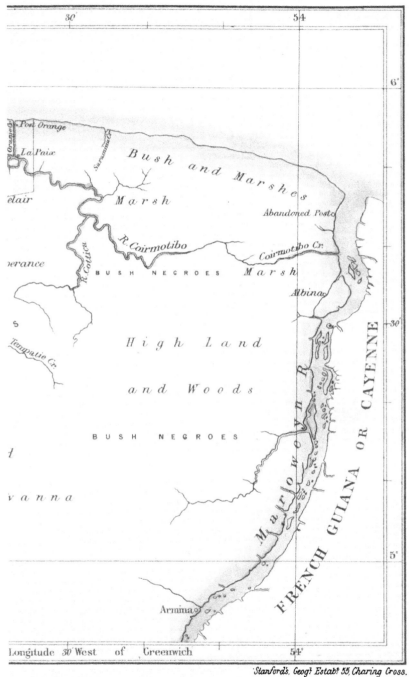

DUTCH GUIANA

BY

W. G. PALGRAVE

AUTHOR OF 'A YEAR'S JOURNEY THROUGH CENTRAL AND EASTERN ARABIA

> "It was a chosen plott of fertile land,—
> As if it had by Nature's cunning hand
> Been choycely picked out from all the rest
> And laid forth for ensample of the best" SPENSER

> "It would be interesting to know the secret of Dutch colonial management, which presents to an outside observer the aspect of minding one's own business, and inducing other people to mind theirs" *Saturday Review*

> "Go to Egypt. It will suit you. I look upon you as an Oriental. If you like, go to South America. Tropical scenery will astonish and cure you" DISRAELI

WITH PLAN AND MAP.

London

MACMILLAN AND CO.

1876

PREFACE.

During my residence in the West Indies, the hospitable instances of my friend, Mr. A. Cohen, at present Her Majesty's Consul for Surinam, seconded by a courteous invitation from his Excellency C. A. van Sypesteyn, Governor of that colony, determined me to pay a visit to Dutch Guiana. My stay there was, of necessity, a short one, not exceeding a fortnight, but during that period the forethought of my amiable hosts had prepared, and put at my disposal, all available means of collecting trustworthy information, both ocular and documentary, regarding the condition of the people and the country. To the kindness of those friends, accordingly, this work owes any interest or value it may possess.

Some inaccuracies, or, at least, some disputable points, may occur in the historical notices scattered through these pages. In the remote station of my present service, I have at hand no means for comparative investigation of the records of the Guiana past; and am compelled, accordingly, to throw myself for such matters on the indulgence of my readers, by whom, if better informed, I shall be thankful to be corrected.

Conversant for many years with the negro races in those Eastern lands where they may be, from long domicilement, regarded as almost indigenous, I have felt a special interest in observing their present condition and probable future in their Western regions of more recent adoption. In no European colony have they been so completely identified with the soil as in Dutch Guiana; nowhere could they be studied to better advantage. To those, therefore, who feel interest, not in African geography only, but in African nationality, I commend the results of my observations on this subject; they are grounded on experience, and ratified by fact.

The Biblical paradise, judging by the records that have come down to us, though not, on the whole, a very progressive, was yet a very pleasant place. Much the same may be said of the Creole paradise—Dutch Guiana. The gates are open: enter.

St. Thomas, W.I.,
  October 24, 1875.

CONTENTS.

MAPS.

Charlesburg

Highroad to Kwatta

Viotte Bridge

Savanna

D

CANAL OF KWATTA

Common Land

D

D

Military

D

Catholic

KEYZER

WEIDE STR

BURENSTR

BRUG

HOOG

VREDE STR

DWARS STR

ZWARTENHOVEN

SARAGA

Moravians
D

Lands-grond

Boniface

NEPVEUS

PONTRENWERF

RUSTEN

HOF STR

GROOTE STR

Highway

GEMEENELANDS

LIMES CANAL

DISTILL

Boat B
Wha.

New Highroad or Millpath

Pleasure Grounds

Mill works

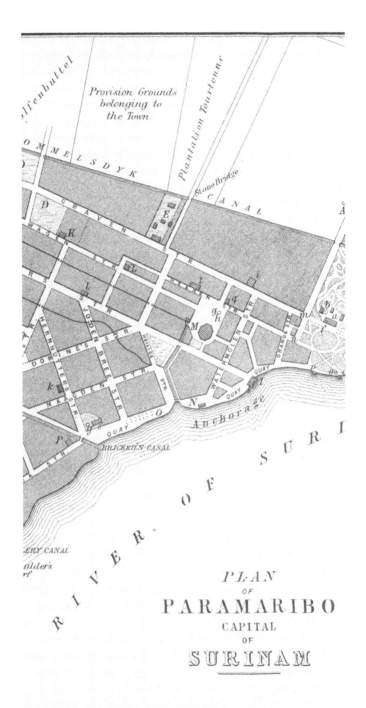

PLAN
OF
PARAMARIBO
CAPITAL
OF
SURINAM

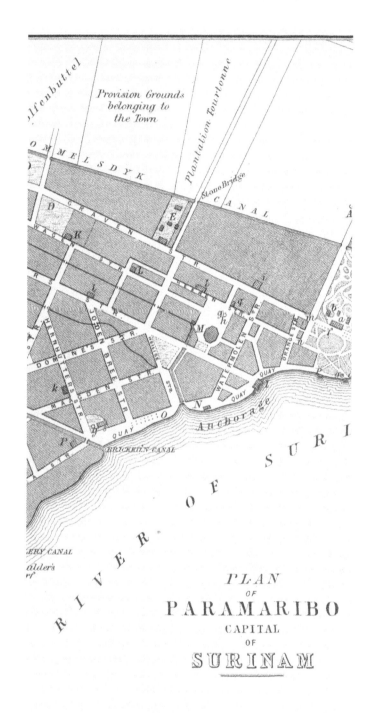

PLAN
OF
PARAMARIBO
CAPITAL
OF
SURINAM

Plantation
Ma Retraite

Cameron
Combé

Fort Zeelandia

N A M

REFERENCE.

A.	Suburb Zeelandia or Combé.	a.	Government House.
B.	Government-house Garden.	b.	Secretary's Quarters.
C.	Garrison Gardens.	c.	Barracks.
D.	Burial Grounds.	d.	Officer's Quarters.
E.	Military Hospital.	e.	Guardroom.
F.	Commandant's Quarters.	f.	Tamarind Avenue.
G.	Engineers Quarters.	g.	Wells.
H.	Military Stores.	h.	Dutch Church.
I.	Weighing Shed.	i.	Catholic Church.
K.	Theatre.	k.	Moravian Church.
L.	Orphanage.	l.	Synagogues.
M.	Militia Guardhouse.	m.	Treasury Buildings.
N.	Police Station.	n.	Law Courts.
O.	Fish Market.	.o.	Jetty.
P.	'Concordia' Masonic Lodge.	p.	Landing Place.
		q.	Club.
		r.	Police Station.
		s.	Lutheran Church.

DUTCH GUIANA.

CHAPTER I.

THE COAST.

> Then creeping carefully along the beach,
> The mouth of a green river did they reach,
> Clearing the sands, and on the yellow bar
> The salt waves and the fresh waves were at war.
>
> MORRIS.

EVERY one who has read—and who has not?—the incomparable story of 'Guy Mannering' knows that the predetermining thread of our existence, whether spun by Meg Merrilies or a Clotho, is, like the life it measures, a many-coloured twine of differing hues. My own particular Clotho, whoever she be, had kindly unreeled for me a fortnight's length, or nearly so, of the very whitest hank ever allotted to mortal, in a region not incorrectly styled by Mr. Anthony Trollope, in his West-Indian reminiscences, the " true and

B

actual Utopia of the Caribbean Seas, namely,
British Guiana"—a region additionally blessed,
at the time of my visit, with that almost Utopian
piece of colonial good fortune, the right man in
the right place, in the person of its present
Governor.

But with British Guiana and the good things
thereof my present tale has, except in the way
of introduction, little to do. George Town and
Berbice, sugar-estates and canals, coolies and
vacuum-pans, hospitable planters and not less
hospitable townsmen, are they not written, and
well written too, in the book above alluded to—
the 'Book of the West Indies and the Spanish
Main'? At any rate I was soon in some manner
acquainted, however superficially, with all these;
and now my principal desire was to acquire some
knowledge of the neighbouring cousin-colony, if
"mother" be not the fitter title—Dutch Guiana.

"'Tis known, at least it should be," that Surinam, geographically indicated by the easterly slice
of Guiana placed between our own South American
possessions, on the one side, and French Cayenne
on the other, is up to the present day under Dutch
rule; while Demerara, or, to speak more correctly,

the broad British territory that includes in one the
three provinces of Berbice, Demerara, and Essequibo, was, till a comparatively recent period,
Dutch also. Now, I had often heard it affirmed
that the immense superstructure of prosperity
raised by British energy on the shores of Demerara owed its oft-tried solidity, if not in whole,
at least in no inconsiderable part, to the well-
devised foundation-work bequeathed us as a
parting legacy by our Batavian predecessors.
Our form of administration is Dutch (so said
my informants), our local institutions Dutch, our
sea-walls are Dutch, our canals, our sluices, the
entire system of irrigation and drainage from
which the land derives its unparalleled fertility,
and we our wealth, all are Dutch. We have made
English use of these things, no doubt, and the
merit of that use is ours; but the merit of the
things themselves is not all our own, it belongs
rather to those who first created them and gave
them to the land.

How far might this be true? Colonial success
amid the many failures recorded, and yet re-
cording in these very regions, must be, every
one will admit, a phenomenon, the sources of

which would be well worth discovery; and here
before me was an instance ready to hand, and a
cause assigned. Why not investigate its correct-
ness? There was time at disposal, and from
George Town to Paramaribo is no great distance. Besides, I had already received assurance of a hearty welcome from his Excellency
Van Sypesteyn, the representative of Dutch
majesty in Surinam; and an invitation of the
sort, when combined with that chiefest of all
factors in life's calculations, juxtaposition, made
the present occasion doubly favourable; so I
readily determined to follow up my Demeraran
visit by another to a region which, while in
natural respects hardly differing for good or evil
from British Guiana, had all along remained
under Batavian mastership, and where, consequently, the original institutions of our own
acquired colony might be conveniently studied,
unmodified, or nearly so, by foreign influences
and change of rule.

From George Town, eastward, an excellent
carriage road runs parallel to the coast, though
at some distance from it inland; the drive is a
pleasant one, traversing a varied succession of

large estates and populous villages, interrupted here and there by patches of marsh and wood, till the journey ends on the western bank of a full-flowing river, the Berbice, beyond which lies the small town of the same name, not far from the Anglo Batavian frontier. Here official kindness had arranged for my further progress, by putting at my disposal the trim little revenue schooner, Gazelle, that now lay at anchor off the lower town-wharf, waiting to take me for a cruise of a hundred and fifty miles—such being the distance interposed between the harbour of Berbice and the mouth of the Surinam river, where rises the capital of Dutch Guiana.

A sailing craft, however small, if in good trim, clean, possessed of a comfortable cabin, and under a steady beam wind, all which advantages were combined in the present instance, is a welcome change from the inevitable smoke, crowding, noise, oily smell, and ceaseless roll of the largest and finest steamer ever propelled by engine. Besides, the circumstances incident to a thirty or forty ton sailing-ship tend to create a friendlier fellow-feeling between passenger and crew than is ordinarily to be met with on her

more business-like rival of three or four thousand
tons; just as a traveller often finds himself more
at home in the modest parlour of a roadside inn
than amid the splendour and bustle of Charing
Cross Hotel or the giant structure of Portland
Place. To sum up, the losses no less than the gains
of steam for those who travel are, after the fashion
of things, much the same by water as by land.
In the present instance, the crew of the Gazelle
was, to a man, composed of creole, that is,
colonial-born negroes; indeed, the pilot's memory reached back to the time when the terms
negro and slave were identical in his own
person, as in the majority of his Guiana brethren.
Civil, cheerful, and obliging as the descendants
of Ham, despite of their ill-conditioned father's
bad example, usually are, they were also —which,
for a voyage like this, amid sand-banks and
shoals, was of more importance—good seamen,
and the captain in charge a good navigator,
though a black one.

"I would rather by any amount have a black
crew than a white one under my orders," is a
remark which I have heard made by many and
many a West Indian sea-captain, lamenting over

the insubordination, drunkenness, and other offences of his men. And in fact negroes, like their half-cousins, the Arabs, have naturally in themselves the making of excellent seamen, active, handy, and daring, besides being far more amenable to the restraints of discipline, and less so to the seductions of the brandy or rum bottle, than the average material of which white crews are, nowadays, formed. And should our own strangely scattered and disunited West Indian possessions ever realize among themselves the ideal "cluster of small states," the not unreasonable hope of other statesmen besides the romantic descendant of the Contarinis, such a confederacy might even more easily recruit her indispensable navy, than her less necessary standing army, from among the black creoles of her own islands and coasts.

A brisk wind was blowing, and the white cloud-drift scudding before the Atlantic trade-wind over the pale blue vault had in it something more akin to a Mediterranean than to a tropical sky, as we weighed anchor, and, taking advantage of the seaward ebb, cleared out of the narrow channel alongside of the low, bush grown shoal that lies athwart the Berbice mouth, and bears, in common with countless other small islets and rocks of these latitudes, the name of Crab Island. The crab here in question is not the dainty crustacean of our seas, but the hideous land-crab known to the students of 'Roderick Random' and 'Tom Cringle'—a monster that may be eaten by such, and such only, as are stomach-proof against the unpleasant associations of burial-grounds and carrion. Soon the tall, formal, semi Batavian houses of Berbice, and its yet taller market-tower or look-out (for every town hereabouts has within its circuit one of these, at least, to serve for a beacon to the seafarer, and a watch-place, whence notice can be given in case of fire or any other sudden danger threatening the townsmen themselves), had disappeared from our view behind river-bend and forest, and by noon we were afloat on the open sea.

The open but "not the blue," much less the typical "black water," of the deep Atlantic. From the Orinoco to the Amazon, the aqueous fringe of the South American coast is a shallow, muddy, brackish, ochrey sort of composition, which overspreads an almost imperceptible

downward slope of alluvial deposit, that reaches
out seaward for ten, fifteen, twenty, or even more
miles, and bears witness to the prodigious volumes
of water poured unceasingly, with little difference
of month or season, by the countless rivers of the
great southern continent into the ocean beyond.
As we slowly made our way up along the coast,
tacking and retacking against the unvarying
trade-breeze, broad gaps in the monotonous line
of low brown forest, the shore-horizon on our left,
successively indicated the mouth of one or other
of these great streams, many among which, nor
those by any means the largest, equal or exceed
the Severn and the Garonne in length of course
and copiousness of flow. Of the latter in particular a further intimation was given by the tossing of our ship where the strong river-current,
felt far out to sea, crossed and thwarted the
regular succession of waves as they rolled slowly
on from the open Atlantic, and roughened them
into whitening breakers.

From the outlet of the Corentyn, that acts as
boundary between British and Dutch Guiana, to
the mouth of the Surinam river itself, hardly
anything beside these wide gaps in the forest

margin, and the corresponding breaker-patches
out at sea, occurs to vary the monotony of yellow
waves and level forest-line, that by its utter sameness wearies the eye and depresses the spirits of
the voyager.

"What a contrast," may that same voyager
not improbably say to himself, "is the Dutch
shore to the coast of British Guiana!" There
the view by sea or land is not particularly picturesque, to be sure; but to make up for the want
of beauty, we have the prospect scarcely less
pleasurable to the mind, if not to the eye, of a
close succession of tall chimneys, each with its
flaunting smoke-pennon, along the whole length
of the southern horizon, from Berbice to the
Pomeroon, or near it, proclaiming an almost continuous cultivation, and the triumphs of the
industry that has transformed a "lonely mud-
bank, once productive of nothing but alligators,
snakes, and mosquitoes," into a thriving, populous,
wealth-coining colony. Here, on the contrary,
not a chimney, not a construction of any sort,
overtops the impenetrable mangrove-growth of
the shore. Scarcely, and at distant intervals, does
an irregular wreath of blue vapour, curling above

the forest, tell its tale of clearing and habitation ;
whence the traveller may, if so minded, deduce
the further conclusion of the inferiority of the
Batavian race to the British, of Dutch colonization
to English, &c.

But this conclusion, like many others drawn at
first sight, would break down on closer inspection
of the premises ; and first of all because the two
coasts, however much alike each other when seen
from five or six miles distance out to sea, are, in
reality, very unlike,—so much so, indeed, that
neither for praise nor blame can any correct com-
parison be made between them. For throughout
the whole, or very nearly the whole, breadth of
British Guiana a wide swamp district, lower itself
than the average sea level, and, in consequence,
very difficult, if not impossible, to drain, cuts off
the available land-strip of the coast itself from the
firm but distant highlands of the interior, and by
so doing confines the choicest sugar-producing
tracts of the colony to the immediate vicinity of
the shore, where they are all arranged side by
side in a long but narrow strip, hemmed in
between the ocean to the north and the almost
equally unmanageable morass on the south. In

Dutch Guiana, on the contrary, a rise, slight but sufficient, of the continental level has thrust forward the swamp-region from the interior down to the very shore, where it forms a barrier, behind which the sugar lands and estates ensconce themselves, with no particular background, until, perhaps, the worthy Brazilians condescend to define their frontier, which, as yet, they seem in no hurry to do, and thus remain, for the most part, out of sight of the seafarer, though not out of easy reach by river communication.

This invisibility from the sea, and those who go down to their business in the great waters, was once by no means an adverse circumstance. On the contrary, it was a very desirable one to the old Dutch settlers throughout the seventeenth and even during the eighteenth century. For those were days when many a gallant Captain Morgan, Captain Trench, or Captain Cutthroat whoever would hail his men on the look-out, as their piratical barque hugged the coast on her way to the golden plunder of the Spanish main, ready enough to shorten sail and let down the boats, had any tempting indication of hoarded Batavian wealth, whether in produce or in coin, appeared within the limits of a long-shore raid. But the case was different so long as the dense bush-barrier defended what it concealed, and the river estuaries, however frequent and wide, afforded no better prospect to the would-be plunderers than that of a difficult and perhaps distant navigation up stream, far from their comrades in the ships at sea, with the additional probabilities of meeting with a fort or two on the way to bar their passage. And thus, throughout the worst days of piratic menace, the hoards of Dutch Guiana remained, with one exception, to be mentioned hereafter, unpillaged, chiefly because unseen; while the more patent treasures of the Frenchman and the Spaniard were harried to enrich the coffers or decorate the Pollies and Betsies of those lawless heroes of the Caribbean deeps.

I said with one exception—a memorable one, from the injury it caused. This was when the more formidable, because the better organized and better supported, buccaneers,—for buccaneers they also were, both in principle and practice, however much they might screen themselves behind royal usage and international law,—Jacques Cassard and De Monans, commanders of the

French squadron, issued from the all too neighbouring ports of Cayenne, to harry the Batavian
settlements within their reach. Had the estates
and factories, the warehouses and stores, of the inland, far up the Surinam, the Commoweyne, and
the Saramacca, been as easy of access to a marine
invader as was the town of Paramaribo itself, (the
more its misfortune), the losses inflicted on Dutch
Guiana by French rapacity in the years 1712,
1713, and 1714 would have been multiplied ten
and twenty fold. Nor was the British flag, so
often a signal of terror and dismay in the Caribbean Archipelago, always a desirable or a friendly
visitant to Dutch shores.

The age of pirates and buccaneers is past, and
even from regular naval invasion a West Indian
colony, under the present circumstances of warfare, has little to fear. But, independently of the
mischief-makers whom of old times it brought on
its waves, the sea of this coast is itself a troublesome and occasionally a dangerous neighbour to
the planter and his labours. Whether it is that
the north-eastern side of this great continent is,
in very truth, slowly sinking, sinking, as runs the
ominous verdict of not a few grave, scientific

judges, or whether, as I found it to be the prevalent opinion among the long-shore men themselves, some secular deflection of winds and
currents yearly brings a heavier volume of water
to war against the unprotected low-lying land, I
know not. But this much is certain, that the sea
encroaches more and more, and that every equi-
noxial spring-tide, in particular, is signalled by a
wider and more perilous invasion of the watery
enemy, and bears his usurpations ever farther
over forest and plain.

Whatever the cause, aqueous or terrene, its
effects are only too certain; and a woeful example
was soon before our eyes, when, after not many
hours' cruise, we anchored off the little town, or,
to speak more truly, remnant of a town, called
Nikarie. The name is, I believe, like most of the
names hereabouts, Indian, the meaning, of course,
unknown. The district, which is also denomi-
nated Nikarie, lies immediately to the east of the
Corentyn river, and is thus the nearest of all to
the British territory. It contains at the present
day, as official returns tell us, nine estates, com-
prising between them 2,832 acres of cultivated soil;
the number was formerly greater, but no portion

of the colony suffered so much from the emancipation crisis, and the other causes of discouragement
and depression, from which wealthier and more
favoured colonies are only now beginning to re-
cover, and that slowly.

The estates, mostly cane or cocoa, are all situated at some distance inland up the river, safely
sheltered behind the tangled mangrove fringe.
Where goods have to be shipped, remoteness from
the sea-coast is, of course, an inconvenience; yet
with this the colonists long preferred to put up,
rather than deviate from their traditionary rule.
But when, at the opening of the present century,
the British lion, jealous lest so choice a morsel as
Dutch Guiana should fall into the jaws of the
ravenous French Republic and still more ravenous
Empire, temporarily extended a protective paw
over these regions, a new order of things prevailed for a time, and an unwonted self-confidence
took, in more than one instance, the place of
prudential caution. Under these novel auspices
the seemingly eligible site of the Nikarie river-
mouth was not likely to be passed over, and soon
a flourishing little town, with streets, shops,
stores, churches, public buildings, and the rest,

arose and dilated itself on the western point, to the great advantage of commerce, and for a while bravely held its own.

But wisdom was, before long, justified of her Batavian children, and the failure of the foreign experiment—a woeful failure—is now almost complete. It was afternoon when we made the port. As we cautiously threaded our way between sandbank and shoal before coming to anchor, we passed a broad, triangular space of shallow water, lashed into seething waves by wind and current, where, a few feet under the surface, lies what was once the busy area of populous streets. Meanwhile, the breakers, not content with the mischief already done, continue ceaselessly tearing away the adjoining land, bit by bit. Right in front, a large house, left an empty shell, without doors or window-frames, by its fugitive inhabitants, is on the point of sinking and disappearing among the waters that, unopposed, wash to and fro through the ground floor. Close by, the victorious sea has invaded the gardens of the neighbouring dwellings, and will evidently soon take possession of the buildings themselves ; their basement work is rotten with the salt spray. Further on, a few

c

isolated fragments of what was once a carefully
constructed sea-dam rise like black specks among
the yeasty waters, and the new earth wall, built
to protect what yet remains of Nikarie, has a
desponding, make-shift look as if aware that it will
not have long to wait for its turn of demolition.
Within its circuit a large, handsome, and solidly
built church, now perilously near the water's
edge, a commodious court-house, where the magistrate of the district presides, a few private dwelling-houses, and three or four grog-shops stand
ranged, like the Maclachlans and Wilsons of the
famous Solway martyr-roll, resignedly awaiting
the steady advance of the tide. The wind was
high, and the roar of the waves, as they burst im-
patiently on the dwindling remnant of what was
once the Nikarie promontory, sounded in the
dusky evening air like a knell of doom.

There are many sad sights in this sad world,
but few give the beholder so dreary a feeling of
helpless melancholy as does a town in the act and
process of being washed away by the sea,—the
forces are so unequal, the destruction so wasteful
and so complete. Fortunately, at Nikarie, however, except for the loss, such as it is, of some acres

of sandbank, and as much building material as
the inhabitants do not think it worth their while
to carry away, no great harm is being done.
Already the situation of a new emporium for the
sugar and other produce of the estate has been
marked out further up the river, and the rise of
the level ground, which is here more rapid than
to the west, along the Demerara coast, will ensure
it, with the adjoining cultivated lands, from any
serious risk of Neptunian invasion for several
years to come. Meanwhile, the spectacle now
presented by Nikarie is undoubtedly a depressing
one to the imagination, if not to the mind, and I
was glad to learn that it was the only one of its
kind on the Surinam coast.

Here first I heard negroes speaking Dutch, and
I have no doubt that they murdered it as ruth-
lessly as they do the Queen's English or the Republic's French elsewhere. But I will not detain
my readers with a minute account of the ways and
fashions of the inhabitants in this Nikarie district,
as we shall have the opportunity of studying
Dutch Guiana life in all its aspects, black, white,
or coloured, to better advantage further on. This,
however, need not hinder our availing ourselves

in the mean time, where convenient, of the information copiously supplied by his Excellency Van Sypesteyn, who was, in youth, the talented historian, as now, in middle age, he is the active and intelligent Governor of Dutch Guiana.

From official documents, it appears that the number of sugar factories in the district of Nikarie is five, all of them worked by steam, and giving an annual result of five or six thousand hogsheads of sugar, besides 60,000 gallons of molasses and about as many puncheons of rum; to which must be added nearly 14,000 pounds weight of coffee and 300,000 of cocoa, from all which data we may safely conclude that the 2,832 acres of its reclaimed land are neither unfruitful nor badly cultivated. Yet the total number of inhabitants only reaches 2,346, more than 600 of whom are Coolie or Chinese emigrants; the remainder are negroes. Here, as elsewhere, under-population is the great stumbling-block in the way of progress.

It is pitiful to think that, out of the 10,000 and more acres, all excellent land, conceded by the Dutch Government to the occupation of the Nikarie proprietors, hardly more than a fourth has been, as the preceding numbers show, brought into actual use. Yet it is neither the climate nor the soil that is here in fault. How often, not in Nikarie and the districts of Surinam, but in St. Vincent, St. Lucia, Trinidad, in almost all these Western Edens, nay, even in flourishing Demerara itself, has the image of little unpicturesque Barbados, unpromising in show, unfavoured by nature, yet thriving, prosperous, over-stocked, and, therefore, only prosperous because over-stocked, recurred to my mind. Improved machinery, Coolies, Chinese, are all of them excellent things, each in their way, but they cannot make up for the absence of that one great requisite of all progress, material or social, a superabundant native population. But how is it to be obtained for our own three-quarters-empty islands? How for Guiana? How for Surinam? Many answers have been given, and more may be given yet; but a wholly satisfactory one is yet to seek. We will try our luck at the solution of this problem further on.

And now our trim little craft is once more on the open sea, bounding from wave to wave, as she cleaves her onward way to the east. Sand-

banks and mud-banks, covered with scarcely more
than a fathom depth of water, kept us out at a considerable distance from the coast; but had we
been nearer we should have had little to study,
except a dull uniform growth of mangrove and
parwa trees, the latter not unlike our own
poplars in shape and foliage. Behind this woody
screen lies the district of Coronie, almost the
only quarter of Dutch Guiana where cotton, once
a favourite speculation, especially about the time
of the late American war, is now grown. So far
as soil and climate are concerned, there is no
assignable reason why it should not be more
widely planted; but agriculture and commerce
have their vagaries, often not less capricious than
those of fashion and dress.

Coronie left behind us, a rougher sea than any
we have yet encountered gives us notice that we
are passing the joint estuary of the Coppename
and Saramacca rivers, each the main artery of
fertile and, comparatively speaking, populous
regions to the south.

Not far inland, by the banks of the Coppename,
though shut out from our sight by the forest
screen, is a settlement bearing the name of

Batavia; and composed exclusively—exception
made, I trust, of the Government inspector and
the doctor—of lepers. A hundred and fifty in
number, they employ themselves in field labour;
have cottages and gardens of their own; and as
the disease is painless, or nearly so, they live on
not unhappily their death in life. The motive
for keeping them thus apart from every one else
is, of course, the idea that their malady is contagious—an idea wide-spread, it is true, but
unsupported by scientific testimony, and probably
due to the horror and disgust excited by the sight
of so loathsome a disorder. Salt fish—the old-
established slave diet throughout the West Indies
—is not improbably responsible in many cases, if
not most, for the disease: though not contagious
and hardly even infectious, it is certainly
hereditary. Improved diet and, above all, fresh
articles of food put a limit to its ravages, and
give hopes that, with proper precautions, it may
ultimately disappear.

For my part, I am not sorry to miss seeing
" Batavia," but I must regret the invisibility of
" Groningen," where, near the mouth of the
Saramacca, a colony of European labourers has

been established for several years past. It is
one of the many attempts made at various times
to supplement negro by European field work, and
has, like the German and Irish colonies of
Jamaica and the Portuguese St. Kitts, proved a
failure in the main; though its inevitable non-
success as a farm has to a certain extent been
compensated by the gardeners and artisans whom
it has supplied to the capital. Something of the
same kind has, I believe, taken place elsewhere.
Field labour and out-door life are things, early or
late, irreconcilable with European vigour, health,
and even existence in the tropical New World.
Nor are they needed there. Of all which, also,
more anon.

A night and a day have passed since we quitted
the melancholy relics of Nikarie; and we are yet
tossing on the turbid waves, several miles from
land. This grows monotonous, and great was
my delight when, on the second evening of our
voyage, just as the brief twilight deepened into
night, we at last sighted, though still at some
distance, the dull gleam of the light-ship,
anchored several miles out to sea, off the mouth
of the Surinam river. Cautiously, for the shoals

are many and the current strong, we made for
the signs of harbour, known even through the
general gloom to our pilot and crew, till, about
midnight, we anchored in smooth water just
within the entry of the mighty stream, here over
three miles in width, and took shelter behind a
long, low, mangrove-covered land-spit running
out from the east.

A wan crescent moon hung dimly over the
black forest-line, and gleamed on the smooth sea-
ward-flowing water, where we lay at anchor,
waiting the rise of the tide, that would not take
place till after daybreak. Not a sign of human
habitation, not a sound of beast or bird; only the
low roar of the breakers outside the bar, and the
ceaseless flapping of the idle rudder against the
sternpost. The air was mild, and no fear of
marsh miasma deterred the crew from taking
their rest where they lay, each prone on his face
along the deck. That negroes always sleep face
downwards is a fact long since observed by Tom
Cringle, or rather Michel Scott, of Jamaican
celebrity; whether his further conjecture, that
this accounts for the flatness of their noses, be
correct, let Darwin decide. Night dews, so much

and so justly dreaded in many parts of the East
Indies, seem to be of little account in these Indies
of the West. This, to venture a guess of my
own in turn, may, perhaps, be owing to the much
lesser degree of variation here occurring between
the diurnal and nocturnal temperature. So we
waited, while our boat's prow pointed steadily
up stream, in a weird solitude, that looked as if
it were the world's outer frontier land, and the
great river the portal to some mysterious and
unexplored regions beyond.

Morning broke at last; the tide turned, and
flowed in, while a fresh breeze, with a sprinkling
of light showers on its wings, blew from the east,
as we hoisted sail for the port of our destination.
Very soon it became evident, from the objects
around us, that the drear loneliness we had just
left behind extended no further than the immediate
margin of the shore, and that we were entering on
a region of industry, prosperity, and life.

What a relief was the change after two days' uniformity of turbid water, with nothing but man-
grove-grown mudbanks for a horizon! With breeze
and tide in our favour we now went briskly on,
while, bend after bend, the river unfolded to our

gaze the treasures that lined its banks, more
varied and more abundant at every turn. Joy-
fully I welcomed first one, then two, then several
tall factory chimneys, each flaunting on the air
its long grey smoke-wreath, silvered in the level
sunbeams; then appeared glimpses of clustered
roofs and brick walls, through the tall trees
planted beside them, boiling-houses, megass-
sheds, distilleries, overseers' dwellings; and not
far removed from each group, rose the tall
gabled roof of the Dutch-built residence for
manager or proprietor, half screened amid the
shades of its garden grove. Factory-chimneys
and distillery-roofs! picturesque objects, indeed!
you say. Yes, my dear Galwegian friend; or if
you hail from the Black Country rather, factory
chimneys and distillery roofs are, I am quite ready
to admit, no very lovely objects when they are
seen grimed with coal smoke, and amid even
grimier surroundings, against the background of
a heavy sepia-coloured sky. But under a bright
sun, mixed up with glittering foliage, overtopped
by graceful palms, and canopied by the most
dazzling of skies, even roofs and chimneys combine with the beauty around them, and become

part of it, in their turn. Or else it was a long
row of cottages, evidently pattern-built, that
announced the presence of Coolies, Indian or
Chinese, and implied the prosperity of those who
could afford to employ such; while the less
regular roof-lines, scattered amid the thick
garden bushes, told of creole or Surinam-born
negro labour. Or roofs and sheds, but without
the accompaniment of factory and chimney, just
visible among the boughs of what the inexperienced
eye might take for a natural-grown forest, mark
the cocoa estate, scarce less lucrative in Surinam
than the cane-field ; or perhaps it is a wide green
expanse of plantain leaves—colossal plantains
these—or the belfry of a Moravian school-house
that shows over the bank ; canoes, too, some mere
hollowed tree-trunks, some of larger construction,
covered barges, six-oar pleasure boats, sloops
with shoulder-of-mutton sails, become more and
more frequent.

So we sailed on, and before long came on one
of the grandest sights that nature affords, the
junction of two mighty rivers. For here, at a
distance of some eight or nine miles from the sea,
the Surinam and the Commeweyne rivers meet

together, the former from the south, the latter
from the east. It was on their united waters
that we had sailed thus far. The Surinam, which
has, like the Demerara, given its name to an
entire region, is navigable by vessels drawing
ten feet of water for a distance of about one
hundred miles up stream ; higher yet, rocks and
rapids permit only canoes to pass. Its sources
lie hid among the forests of the equatorial
mountain-land that forms the watershed of the
valley of the Amazon, four or five degrees
further still to the south; its breadth for the last
forty miles, before junction with the Commeweyne,
averages above half a mile, its depth from thirty
to sixty feet. It is the main artery of the colony,
which, indeed was for many years limited to the
immediate neighbourhood of its banks. The
Commeweyne of shorter course, but here, at the
junction point, little, if at all, inferior in breadth
and depth to the Surinam itself, runs on an inland
parallel with the eastern coast for a distance of
some forty miles ; further up, a number of smaller
rivers, the Cottica, the Perica, the Coermoeribo,
and others, deep though narrow streams, unite
their waters to form the main trunk.

On the point which divides the two great rivers, a Hindoo ruler of the good old times, and before the unkind interference of a low-caste Government had, Paul-like, commanded widows rather to marry than to burn, would doubtless have erected a graceful temple, and consecrated the spot to the decorous performance of suttee; Dutch Governors, a more practical style of men, utilized the spot by erecting on it the fortress of " New Amsterdam." Its first stone was laid in 1734, shortly after the plundering exploits of Cassard and the French squadron; its object was evidently the protection of the capital from any repetitions of the like visits in future. But though Paramaribo and New Amsterdam, too, have since that date twice received French, twice English masters within their walls, it has so happened that the fort guns have never had occasion to pour forth any more deadly fire than that of a signal or a salute, treaties having in later times subjected the colony to those changes that hard fighting brought about in former days. However, the position of New Amsterdam is well chosen, the works strong, and should any future age raise up against the Dutch colonies a new

Cassard, he would find in the batteries enough and more than enough to render a buccaneering excursion up to Paramaribo by no means so easy a business as of yore.

We saluted the national flag, and, passing close under a very respectable battery, exchanged a few words of amicable Dutch with a subaltern, who, at the sight of our Government pennon, had hastened down for inquiry to the water's edge. Exempted by his courtesy—a courtesy I have never found wanting in any of his Batavian comrades—from the delays of an inspectorial visit, we continued our course due south, up the Surinam river; but the breeze had died away, and it was near noon when, after about eight miles of slow progress between banks and scenes much like those already described, but with a continually increasing denseness of estates and cultivation on either side, we approached the capital. Gardens too, small dwelling-houses, and crowded cottages rose thicker and thicker into view ; a tall Flemish-looking tower glittered in the sun, and, at last, rounding an abrupt fort-crowned promontory on the left river bank, we cast anchor opposite the river quay and townhall of Paramaribo.

CHAPTER II.

THE CAPITAL.

In the afternoon they came unto a land
In which it seemed always afternoon.

TENNYSON.

IT was not afternoon, in fact it was forenoon,
and the sun, though mounted high, had not yet
throned himself in his meridian tower, when,
accompanied by those who had come to meet and
welcome my arrival, I mounted a red brick flight
of steps, leading from the water's edge up to the
raised quay, and found myself on the threshold
of the capital of Dutch Surinam. Yet there was
something in the atmosphere that can only be
described as post-meridian—an influence extending over everything around, town and people
alike; nor post-meridian only, but distinctly
lotophagous, befitting the lotus-eating capital of
a lotus-eating land, very calm and still, yet very
comfortable and desirable withal.

For what regards the material atmosphere, its
heavy warmth, even at so early an hour as ten or
eleven of the morning, need excite no surprise.
Paramaribo stands on the South American map at
little more than five and a half degrees north of
the equator, and the equator here crosses the
immense breadth of the moist plains, brimming
river-meshes, and dense forests that constitute
nine-tenths of the Guianas and Brazil. Fifteen
miles, at least, in a straight line, removed from
the nearest coast, and cut off from the very
limited sea-breeze of the tropics by intervening
belts of plantation and thick wood, the air of
Paramaribo is not that of wind-swept Barbados
or dry Antigua, but that of the moistest among
all equatorial continents, and may best be
likened to the air of an orchid-house at Kew and
that of a Turkish bath combined. Not, be it
well understood, a dry-heated, pseudo-Turkish
bath of the European kind, but a genuine ham-
mam of Damascus or Constantinople. In such
an atmosphere, Ulysses himself and his crew must
after a very short stay have betaken themselves
in company with the natives to lotus-eating ; it is
a duty imposed by the climate, and there are

D

many less agreeable duties in the world elsewhere.

Not that the climate is unhealthy; quite the
reverse. That tall, large-made, elderly European
gentleman in a light grey suit, who, parasol in
hand, grandly saunters by, evidently does so
not from any want of vigour, either in mind or
limb, but because a sauntering step is more congenial to the place than a brisk one; those sleek,
stout, comfortable, glossy negroes, loitering in
sun or shade, appear, and are, in fact, equal, did
the occasion require it, to any exertion of which
human muscle is capable; they are doing nothing
in particular, because nothing in particular is just
now the proper thing to do. The town itself, its
tall houses, its wide streets, its gardens, its
squares, its shady avenues, its lofty watch-tower,
its tree-embosomed palace, its shrub-embosomed
cottages, each and every particular of the scene,
animate or inanimate, is stamped with the same
character. " Take it easy," seems the lesson they
all alike inculcate; and the lesson is a popular
one, soon learnt, and steadily practised on every
hand.

But appearances, however real for what regards

the surface of which they are part, may yet be
very deceptive, if reasoned from unconditionally
to what exists beneath them ; and a town that
numbers more than 22,000 inhabitants, itself the
capital of a colony that yearly exports to the
average value of a third of a million sterling, cannot
be wholly peopled by dreamy lotus-eaters, delicious
lotus-eaters only ; nor can the sole occupation of
the dwellers in city or field be lotus-eating, either
physical or moral.

The solid and underlying fact of Paramaribo
is that, amid this atmosphere and on this segment
of the great Guiana delta, have planted themselves and taken root, no longer exotic but
indigenous, the same Dutch industry, Dutch
perseverance, and Dutch good sense that of old
turned the sandy swamps of the Batavian delta
into a flower-garden, and erected the Venice of
the North on the storm-swept shores of the
Zuider Zee. Surinam, rightly understood, is
only Holland under another sky ; Paramaribo is
Amsterdam by other waters : the colouring and
toning of the picture may indeed be equatorial
Creole, but the lines and grouping are those of the
Netherlands school, and no other.

D 2

This it is that gives to Paramaribo its twofold character, at once European and tropical, Dutch and Creole—a blending of opposites, a dual uniformity—an aspect that, when first beheld, leaves on the mind an impression bordering on unreality, as if place and people were imaged in a hot, picturesque dream. Yet Paramaribo is no dream, nor its inhabitants dream-shapes; very much the contrary. In fact, no capital town throughout the West Indies, no offspring of European stem, French, English, Danish, or even Spanish, so genuinely, so truthfully, represents the colony to which it belongs as Dutch Paramaribo. Contrary examples are easily adduced. Thus, for instance, Jamaica is pre-eminently the land of English country gentlemen, of magistrates, landlords, farmers, and, in tone, ways, and life, an English country district; while Demerara is in no small measure an English or, rather, I should say, a Scotch manufacturing district; Barbados, an English parish (Little Pedlington its satirists, of whom I beg to state that I am not one, would call it) magnified into an island. But neither Jamaica nor Demerara nor Barbados possesses a correct epitome of itself in Kingston, Georgetown, or

even Bridgetown: each of these three seaports
has a character of its own, distinct from, and in
some respects opposed to, the colony at large.
This is due to many causes, and, most of all, to
the "mixed multitude" of trade, the camp-fol-
lowers of enterprise, who, under whatever banner
they congregate, acknowledge in heart and life
no flag but that of individual self-interest. These
are they who muster strongest in the generality
of colonial towns, especially seaports, and tinge,
if they do not absolutely colour, the places of their
resort. And thus from the merest port of call
along these shores, where the "condottiere"
element is at its maximum, to Georgetown, where
it is decidedly at its minimum, a something of a
restless, make-shift, egotistic, "cheap-Jack" admixture obscures, or at least jars with, the public-
spirited nationality, unsettles the population,
debases the buildings, ungroups the unity, and
deforms the beauty of place and site.

With Paramaribo it is otherwise. The broad,
straight streets, flanked with spacious and lofty
houses, shaded by carefully planted avenues,
adorned with public buildings that Scheveningen
or the Hague need not blush to own, and trim

almost as the waysides of Brock; the Governor's
residence, a miniature palace for elegance of
style and stately appearance; the spacious Ma-
sonic lodge, "Concordia," where a Grand Orient
himself—I speak as a profane, and, if the term
be incorrect, apologize—might hold his assembly;
the seemly synagogues—Dutch the one, Portuguese the other; the decorous if somewhat heavy-
built churches, reformed and Lutheran; the
lighter constructed but more spacious establishments, Moravian and Catholic; the lofty Town
Hall, with its loftier tower, that from a hundred
and twenty feet of height looks down over fort
and river; the Court-house hard by; the noble
Military Hospital, with its wide verandahs, open
staircases, and cool halls; the strong-built Fort
and Barracks; the Theatre, the Club-house, the
many other buildings of public use and ornament,
—all these are Dutch in appearance and character
—all expressive of the Eleven Provinces, though
chiefly of Zeeland and the steady purpose of her
sons. The well-planned and carefully kept
canals that intersect the town in every direction,
the neat bridges, the broad river-side quays, the
trim gardens, the decent cemeteries, the entire

order and disposition of the place, tell the same
tale, witness to the same founders, reflect the
same image, true to its original on the North
Sea coast: all tell of settled order and tasteful
method.

Is there in Dutch—for there certainly exists
not in English—a guide-book of the town of
Paramaribo, capital of Dutch Surinam? Perhaps
there is; but I have not had the fortune to see it.
However that may be, I must run the risk implied in writing as if of things familiar to every
one, though, in fact, Paramaribo and Surinam
may very possibly be not much better known
to the good folks of Amsterdam and Rotterdam
in general, let alone those of London or Norwich,
than are the districts of Timboo and the town of
Timbuctoo. Bearing this in mind, I think that
a brief historical notice and an equally brief
topographical description of the Surinam capital,
and incidentally of the colony at large, will,
under circumstances like these, hardly stand in
need of an apology. There is little profit in
reading of travels, or in making them, unless
they be prefaced by some knowledge of the
countries and their inhabitants: the former may

best be studied in their maps; the latter in their histories.

Revealed to Europe in 1499 by the great discoverer who gave his name to the American continent, Surinam, like the rest of the North-Guiana delta, though visited by adventurers of almost every nationality, remained for more than a century unclaimed, because uncolonized by any. Gradually, however, the future triple division of this part of the coast-region began to foreshadow itself in the marked persistency of English, French, and Dutch enterprise, all of which together contributed to the foundation of the Surinam settlement, though the honour of having first introduced regular land-cultivation, and erected a fort, belongs not to a Dutch but an English captain, whose name is borne by the little watercourse called Marshall's creek, a tributary stream of the Surinam river, or, as it was then called, the Greater Coma, some sixty or seventy miles' distance from the sea. But Thoracica, the spot selected by Marshall in 1603, was not destined long to enjoy its metropolitan honours; and the Indian village of Paramaribo, where a settlement had already been made by French emigrants as early, some say, as

1640, was by Lord Willoughby of Parham raised
to the dignity of capital, in 1650—a dignity
which it retained when, a few years later, it
passed definitively under the Dutch flag. The
name itself, "Paramaribo," is of Indian origin,
not a derivative of "Parham," as some have
erroneously stated.

The site was well chosen. The Surinam, here
a tidal river of nearly a mile broad, flows past
a slightly raised plateau of sand and gravel
mixed with "caddy," a compound of finely
broken fragments of shell and coral, extending
for some distance along the left or west bank.
The general elevation of the ground is about six-
teen feet above low-water level, enough to insure
it from being overflowed in the rainy seasons or by
the highest tides. Several streams, improved by
Dutch industry into canals, intersect this level;
one of them connects the waters of the Surinam
with those of the Saramacca further west : all are
tidal in their ebb and flow. Drainage is thus
rendered easy; and, now that the low bush and
scrub, the natural growth of every South
American soil, however light, has been cleared
away, the citizens of Paramaribo may securely

boast that throughout the entire extent of Guiana, from the Oronoco to the Amazon, no healthier town than theirs is to be found.

This healthiness is, however, in great measure due to their own exertions; and above all to the good sense that presided over the construction of the town. When the true founder of town and colony alike, Cornelius van Aerssen, Lord of Sommelsdyk, and the fifth Governor of Dutch Guiana, landed on these shores in 1683, Paramaribo—so he wrote—consisted of only " twenty-seven dwellings, more than half of which were grog-shops," and close to it the Fort of Zeelandia, so named after its builders, the intrepid Zeelanders, who had already repelled more than one Indian or English assault from its walls. But under the vigorous administration of Sommelsdyk the rapidly rising prosperity of the colony was reflected in the town itself, that henceforth grew and prospered year by year. Its records describe it in 1750 as already covering one-half of its present extent; and, in 1790, the number of houses within its circuit exceeded a thousand; till, about the beginning of the present century, the addition of the extensive suburb of " Combe," on the north side, brought it up to its actual limits. Then followed a long and dreary period of colonial depression, general, indeed, throughout the West Indies, but nowhere (Jamaica perhaps excepted) greater than in Surinam, where the uncertainty consequent on a reiterated change of masters, French, English, and Dutch, helped to depreciate the already declining value of estates and produce in this part of the world. Misfortunes never come singly ; and, while the colony at large suffered, Paramaribo in particular, ravaged by two severe conflagrations, the one in 1821 and the other in 1832, presented a melancholy spectacle of unrepaired ruins and abandoned suburbs. Between 1840 and 1860 things were at their worst, both for colony and capital. Then came the turn : the shock of emancipation passed, its benefits remained; town and country alike revived together; houses were rebuilt, suburbs repopulated ; and of her past wounds the Paramaribo of our day now scarcely shows a scar. The number of her inhabitants, reckoned at barely 16,000 in 1854, at present exceeds 22,000, thus showing an increase of 6,000 in the course of the last twenty years only.

" A goodly city is this Antium ," but during
the hot hours of the day, that is, from eight or at
latest nine in the morning till pretty near sunset,
I would not willingly incur the responsibility of
sending a friend, or even an enemy, unless he
happened to be a mortal one, on a sight-seeing
stroll through the streets of Paramaribo Car-
riages or riding-horses there are few to be found
in the town, and none at all for hire. Negro
carts are plenty, to be sure, and negro mules, too;
but the former, independently of other consider-
ations, are jolting conveyances; the latter a hard-
mouthed, stiff-necked generation; and neither
adapted to the furtherance of European loco-
motion, whether on pleasure or business. As to
walking exercise under this equatorial sun, it
might possibly be an agreeable recreation for a
salamander, but hardly for any other creature.

It is true that shade may be found even in the
hottest hours of perpendicular noon; and when
the sun has fairly beaten you (as he will in less
than five minutes) from the field, you may take
refuge, if you choose, under the broad-leaved,
glistering, umbrella-like almond-trees—so called
from a superficial resemblance between the

kernels of their fruit and those of the almond,
but neither in foliage nor growth having the most
distant likeness to the European tree of that
name—which Dutch forethought has kindly
planted all along the river-quay. There, in
company with any number of ragged black
loungers, you may improve your leisure by
watching the great barges as they float leisurely
along the tide, bearing their neatly protected
loads of sugar, cocoa, or other plantation produce
for the cargo-ships that wait off the town-
" stellings " or wharfs, patiently moored day
by day, with so little bustle or movement of life
about them, that you wonder whether their
crews have not all by common consent abandoned
them and gone off to join a lotus-eating majority
on shore. Or, if you are driven to seek refuge
while wandering through the interior of the
town, the great broad streets, all mathematically
straight, will offer you the shelter of their noble
avenues, where tamarind, mahogany, sand box,
or other leafy trees, planted with Batavian regu-
larity, cast down a long black streak of shade on
the glaring whiteness of the highway. Or you
may rest, if so inclined, beside some well in one

of the many rectangular spaces left open, for the sake of air or ornament, here and there in the very heart of the town, like squares in London, but without the soot.

One such green oasis contains, half hidden amid its trees, the handsome Portuguese Synagogue of recent construction; another, the Dutch, less showy, but more substantial, as befits the old standing and wealth of the worshippers within its walls, and the memory of Samuel Cohen Nassy, its talented founder—the Surinam Joshua of his tribe, when they camped, two centuries ago, on the banks of their newly acquired Jordan. A third "square" (I use the inappropriate word for want of a better in our own language, but the French "place" or Arab "meidan" would more correctly express the thing) boasts the presence of the Dutch Reformed Church—the building, I mean—a model of heavy propriety, suggestive of pew-openers and the Hundredth Psalm, Old Tune; while a fourth has in its enclosure the flimsy, all-for-show construction that does appropriate duty for the gaudy rites of Rome. A fifth has for its centre-piece the Lutheran place of worship; a sixth, the

Moravian; and so forth. But, whatever be the
gods within, the surroundings of every temple
are of a kind in which Mr. Tylor could legiti-
mately discern something of a "survival" of
tree-worship and the "groves" of old—a sensible
survival in these sun-lorded equatorial regions.
Select, then, your city of refuge where you will;
but except it be by chance some stray black
policeman, whom an unusual and utterly heroic
sense of duty keeps awake and on his beat, or a
few dust-sprinkled ebony children, too young as
yet to appreciate the impropriety of being up
and alive at this hour, you yourself and the un-
gainly Johnny-crows that here, as at Kingston,
do an acknowledged share of the street-cleaning
business, will be the only animal specimens dis-
cernible among this profusion of vegetable life.
For these shade-spots, with all their cool, are
delusive in their promise. They are mere islets
plunged amid an overwhelming ocean of light
and heat; and flesh, however solid, though protected by them from actual combustion in the
furnace around, must soon thaw and resolve
itself into a dew under the influence of the
reflected glare.

Better take example, as indeed it is the traveller's wisdom to do in any latitude, whether
tropical or arctic, from the natives of the land,
and like them retire, after a substantial one
o'clock breakfast, luncheon, or dinner,—since
any of these three designations may be fairly
applied to the meal in question,—to an easy
undress and quiet slumber till four, or later,
have "chappit" in the afternoon. In doors
you will find it cool enough. The house walls,
though of wood, at least throughout the upper
stories, are solidly constructed, and are further
protected from the heat by any amount of
verandahs outside, which in true Dutch taste are
not rarely dissembled under the architectural
appearance of porticos; the house-roofs are highly
pitched, and an airy attic intervenes between
them and the habitation below; the windows too
are well furnished with jalousies and shutters;
and the bedrooms are most often up two flights
of stairs—occasionally three. If, under circumstances like these, you cannot keep cool, especially
when you have nothing else on earth to do,
you have only yourself, not the climate, to
blame. Such at any rate is the opinion, con-

firmed by practice, of the colonists universally,
European or creole, white or coloured; and as
they have in fact been up and at work, each in his
particular line of business, ever since earliest
dawn, it would be hard to grudge them their
stated and, for the matter of that, well-earned
afternoon nap. Merchants, tradesmen, account-
ants, proprietors, bankers, and the like, thus disposed of, his Dutch Majesty's officials, civil,
military, or naval (for a small frigate is always
stationed at Paramaribo, ready at the Colonial
Governor's behests), may, I think, sleep securely
calm when all around are sleeping; nay, even the
watchmen—and they are many in these gates
of keen energetic Israel—have retired to their
tents in the universal post-meridian trance. As
to the 18,000 or 19,000 negroes of the town, it
would be superfluous to say that no special
persuasion or inducement of local custom is
needed to induce *them* to sleep, either at this
or any other hour of the day.

Follow, then, the leader or rather the whole
band. If, however, you still prefer to prove
yourself a stranger by using your eyes for sight-
seeing at a time when every genuine Para-

E

mariban has closed his for sleep, the open parade-
ground will afford you, while crossing it, an
excellent opportunity for experimental apprecia-
tion of the intensity of the solar rays, lat. 5° 40″
north. This done you may, or rather you
certainly will, take speedy refuge under the noble
overarching tamarind alley that leads up from
the parade-ground to the front of Government
House; and passing through the cool and lofty
hall of the building, left open, West India
fashion, to every comer, make your way into the
garden, or rather park, that lies behind. It is
probable that the peccaries, tapirs, monkeys,
deer, and the other animal beauties or monstro-
sities, collected the most of them by his Excellency the present Governor, and domiciled in
ample wire inclosures between the flower-beds,
will, in their quality of natives, be fast asleep;
and if the quaint, noisy, screaming birds, the
tamed representatives of Guiana ornithology,
collected here are asleep also, you may admire
their plumage without needing to regret the
muteness of their " most sweet voices." But the
humming-birds and butterflies are wide awake,
and, unalarmed by your approach, will continue

to busy themselves among flowers, such as Van
Elst himself never painted, nor Spenser sung:
here is a crimson passion-flower, there a pink-
streaked lily; golden clusters hang from one
plant, spikes of dazzling blue rise from another;
the humming-birds themselves are only dis-
tinguishable from them as they dart through
by the metallic lustre, not by the vividness or
variety, of their colours. As to the butterflies,
who is the greatest admirer of the race?
Mr. Wallace, I think: let him see the butterflies
of Surinam, and die. Beyond this, the flower-
garden merges in the park—a Guiana park of
Guiana trees: their names and qualities it is easy
to look out in books, or recapitulate from
memory. But how to describe them as they are?
Mr. Ruskin says, that the tree-designer begins
by finding his work difficult, and ends by finding
it impossible; and I say the same of the tree-
describer, at any rate here. And yet luxuriant as
is the Government House garden, I am not sure
if any of its beauties charmed me so much as the
exquisite betel-nut avenue, each palm averaging
fifty feet in height, and each equally perfect in
form and colour, that adorns the central space

enclosed by the spacious buildings of the public
hospital at the further end of the town. Leave
all these if you can, and, which will be better
still, enter instead the cool vaulted brick hall
of genuine Dutch burgher build, that serves
partly as an entry to the public law offices and
courts, partly as a depository for whatever
colonial records have escaped the destructive fires
of '21 and '32.

Hence you may mount, but leisurely, in com-
passion for your guide if not for yourself, the
central tower, till you reach the lantern-like construction, that at a height of 100 feet crowns
the summit of the Town Hall. There stand and
look down far and wide over the most fertile
plain that ever alluvial deposit formed in the
New World or the Old either. On every side
extends a green tree-grown level as far as the eye
can reach; its surface just high enough raised
above water-mark to escape becoming a swamp,
yet nowhere too high for easy irrigation;
capriciously marked at frequent intervals by
shining silver dashes, that indicate sometimes the
winding of rivers broad and deep, sometimes the
more regular lines of canals, of creeks, and of all

the innumerable waterways which in this region
supply the want of roads, and give access to
every district that lies between the northern
sea and the equatorial watershed, far beyond the
limits of European enterprise, all too narrow as
yet. Long years must pass before the children of
Surinam have cause to complain that the "place
is too strait for them"; long before the cultivation that now forms an emerald ring of excep-
tional brightness round the city, and reaches out
in radiating lines and interrupted patches along
the courses of the giant rivers, has filled up
the entire land circle visible from the Tower of
Paramaribo alone.

The day has declined from heat to heat, and
at last the tall trees begin to intercept the slant
sun-rays; when, behold! with one consent Paramaribo, high and low, awakes, shakes itself, puts
on its clothes, ragged or gay, and comes out to
open air and life. The chief place of resort is, of
course, the parade-ground, where, according to
established custom, a Dutch or creole military
band performs twice a week, and where, in the
absence of musical attractions, cool air, pleasant
walks, free views, and the neighbourhood of the

river draw crowds of loungers, especially of the
middle and even upper classes. But, in truth,
for a couple of hours, or near it, every road, every
street, is full of comers and goers, and loud with
talk and laughter. For the negro element, a
noisy one, predominates over all, even within the
capital itself; the Dutch, though rulers of the
land, are few, and other Europeans fewer still.
Indeed, a late census gave the total number of
whites in the town, the soldiers of the fort included,
but little over a thousand. As to Indians, the
pure-blooded ones of their kind have long since
abandoned the neighbourhood of Paramaribo,
and now seldom revisit the locality to which two
centuries past they gave a name: a few half-
breeds, with broad oval faces and straight black
hair, alone represent the race. Bush negroes, in
genuine African nudity, may be seen in plenty
from the river-wharves; but they seldom leave
their floating houses and barges to venture on
shore, though common sense has for some time
past relaxed the prudish regulations of former
times, according to which no unbreeched male
or unpetticoated female was permitted to shock
the decorum of Paramaribo promenades. Coolies

and Chinese, too, though now tolerably numerous on the estates, where, indeed, about 5,000 of them are employed, are rarely to be met with in the streets of the capital; which in this respect offers a remarkable contrast to Georgetown and Port of Spain, where the mild Hindoo meets you at every turning with that ineffable air of mixed self-importance and servility that a Hindoo alone can assume, and China men and women make day hideous with the preternatural ugliness of what flattery alone can term their features. The absence of these beauties here may be explained partly by the recentness of their introduction into the Dutch colony, where they are still bound by their first indentures to field-work, and consequently unable as yet to display their shopkeeping talents; partly by the number and activity of the negro creole population, which has preoccupied every city berth. Of all strangers, only the irrepressible Barbadian, with the insular characteristics of his kind fresh about him, has made good his footing among the Surinam grog-shops and wharfs, where he asserts the position due to his ready-handed energy, and keeps it too. But the diversity between the Barbados negro and his kinsmen of the neighbouring islands or of the Main is one rather of expression and voice than of clothes and general bearing, and hence may readily pass unnoticed in the general aspect of a crowd.

"Aim at consistency," has said one of the foremost ethical teachers of our own or indeed of any time. Were John Henry Newman by the strangest of all strange chances ever to visit Paramaribo, he would, I think, allow that both town and its inhabitants do not come far short in this respect of his standard of excellence. He might wander at night when the snow-like dazzle of the pure moonbeams lights up the tall house-fronts and rectilinear streets in ghostly loneliness, or at the scarcely less lonely hour of noon, when the shrunk shadows disappear in the perpendicular blaze, and in either scene admire the uniform consistency of idea which has impressed on every dwelling, from the tiniest creole cottage up to the princely residence of Government, the same general character of comfort, good taste, and a certain decorous refinement, content with what it has attained, and expressive, if not of progress, of stability, order, and calm. The architectural

jumble, indicative of restless and incongruous
tendencies, that has in so many other colonial
towns erected Gothic, or quasi-Gothic, churches
and church towers amid the flat lines of low-
roofed bungalows, or thrust a Venetian-palace
front into the midst of palms and mango-trees,
offends not here Churches, houses, buildings,
bridges, quays, streets, squares, all are the same
in kind, though differing in scale; all in accord
with each other, and with the climate too.

But if, during the busy morning hours, or in
the idle eventide, our Littlemore ethicist were to
survey the same streets crowded with passers-by
of every class and colour, he would, so soon as
his eye had learnt to penetrate beneath the motley
surface of seeming incongruities, acknowledge the
praise of consistency as due to the inhabitants of
Paramaribo not less than to the material town
itself. However diversified the species, the
genus is one. Watch the throng as it passes—
the kerchief turbaned, loose-garmented market-
women—the ragged porter, and yet more ragged
boatman—the gardener, with his cartful of yams,
bananas, sweet potatoes, and so forth—the white-
clad shop-clerk and writer, the straw-hatted

salesman, the umbrella-bearing merchant—sailors,
soldiers, policemen, quaintly dressed as policemen
are by prescriptive right everywhere, except in
sensible, practical Demerara—officials, aides-de-
camp, high and low, rich and poor, one with
another—and you will see that, through and above
this variety of dress, occupation, rank, colour
even, there runs a certain uniformity of character,
a something in which all participate, from first to
last.

A few exceptions indeed there are, but they
are confined almost exclusively to the white
colonists, and among them even the anomalies
are few. In general, one pattern comprehends the
entire category of white colonists, men and
women, gentle and simple; and it is an eminently
self-contained, self-consistent pattern—the Dutch.
Steady in business, methodical in habit, econo-
mical in expenditure, liberal in outlay, hospitable
in entertainment, cheerful without flightiness,
kindly without affectation, serious without dul-
ness, no one acquainted, even moderately, with
the mother country can fail to recognize the
genuine type of the Hague in the colonial official,
and that of Maestricht or Amsterdam in the busi-

ness population of Paramaribo. This, indeed,
might have been fairly anticipated, the steady,
unimpressionable Dutchman being less subject to
—what shall we call it?—equatorization than the
soon-demoralized Spaniard or lighter Portuguese.
It is a matter of more surprise, an agreeable surprise, when we find much that recalls to mind the
Dutch peasantry and labouring classes distinctly
traceable among the corresponding classes of
creole negroes throughout the delta of Surinam.
By what influence is it—attraction, sympathy,
or mastership?—that some nations so eminently
succeed in transforming the acquired subjects of
whatever race into copies and, occasionally, cari-
catures of themselves, while other nations not less
signally fail in doing so? That Frenchmen,
however much they may annoy those they annex
by their incurable habit of administrative over-
meddling, yet make, not always, indeed,
obedient subjects of France, but, anyhow,
Frenchmen and Frenchwomen out of those they
rule, is a fact attested everywhere, and one that
will long remain to show German eyes and grieve
German hearts in Alsace and Lorraine. How
long ago is it since the Tricolor has been hauled

down to make place for the Union Jack at St. Lucia, St. Vincent, Dominica, and Trinidad? Yet in each of these and their kindred isles, the French impress still survives, uneffaced, as yet, by change and time. Much in the same way, to run through the list of other national annexations or conquests, Brazil is not merely ruled by a Portuguese emperor, but is Portuguese itself; and even the revolted Spanish colonies are Spanish in almost everything but official allegiance, to this day. On the contrary, who ever heard of a land Germanized by the Germans, however influential their settlers, and absolute their rule? And is there the remotest prospect that the Hindoo, though reconciled by sheer self-interest to toleration of the most equitable rule that ever race exercised over race, will ever become, not merely an English subject, but an Englishman in ways and heart? Still more complete has been the failure of Danish attempts at extra-national assimilation in whatever land or age, from the days of Æthelred to our own. But, indeed, where there is diversity of blood, mistrust and antipathy are more easily accounted for than sympathy and unison. To return to our Dutch friends: how it may be

with them elsewhere—in Java, for instance—I
know not; here, on the Guiana coast, they have
almost outdone the French in assimilative results—
a problem of which the solution must be sought,
partly in history, partly in actual observation.
Our best opportunity for the latter will be when
visiting the country districts further up the river,
among the estates.

Meanwhile, let us linger yet a little in Paramaribo itself; and here among the European
townsmen their visitor will find everywhere, so
he be one that deserve to find, a pleasant uniformity of unostentatious but cordial welcome, of
liberal entertainment, of thoughtful and rational
hospitality, attentive to the physical and not neg-
lectful of the mental requirements of the guest
—whatever, in a word, he would meet with,
though under a different aspect, on the shores of
the Yssel or the Waal. Indeed, he might even
have some difficulty in remembering, when en-
deavouring to recall to mind the events of his
stay in the Surinam capital, at which citizen's
house in particular he passed that pleasant
evening; at whose table he shared that copious
meal, breakfast, dinner, or supper; where it was

that he admired the fine old china and massive
plate; under which roof the hostess smiled most
courteously, the host conversed with most good
nature and good sense. After all, " *si vis ut reda-
meris ama*" holds good in every age and land;
and if the Dutch colonists and creoles of Surinam
are universally popular, it is because they have
been at the pains of earning popularity, which,
like other good things, has its price, and is worth
it too.

Much the same, proportion and circumstances
taken into account, may be said of the black
creoles of Dutch Guiana. The evils and degradation inseparable from slavery were not, it is
true, wanting here; but, in spite of these unfa-
vourable antecedents, the Surinam negro has
amply proved by his conduct, both before and
during emancipation, that he had learnt from his
white masters lessons of steadiness, of order, of
self-respect, of quiet industry, of kindliness even,
not indeed alien from his own native character,
but too often unpractised elsewhere. And thus
the ex-slave has, with a rapidity of change to
which, I believe, no parallel can be found in the
history of any other West Indian colony, blended

into national and even, within certain limits,
into social unison with his masters—a unison so
little impaired by the inevitable, however invo-
luntary, rivalry consequent on differences, some
artificial, indeed, but some immanent, of caste
and race, as to afford the best hopes for the
future of the entire colony. It is remarkable
that even the terrible servile wars, which lasted
with hardly an interruption for sixty entire years
—that is, from 1715 to 1775—and not only
checked the prosperity, but even more than once
menaced the very existence of the colony, should
have passed and left behind them no trace, however slight, of hostile feeling or memory among
the negro population, whether slave or free; that
no outbreak, like those of Jamaica, Sainte Croix,
and so many other neighbouring colonies, here
followed or anticipated emancipation, though de-
layed in Surinam till 1863; and, more remarkable yet, that no discontent interfered with
the compulsory though paid labour of the ten
years following. Slavery quietly faded into
apprenticeship; apprenticeship into freedom; and
in a land where riot and revolt would have a
better chance than anywhere else of success, that

chance was never embodied in act. Facts like
these speak certainly well for the creole blacks;
but, if attentively considered, they speak even
better in favour of their white masters. Our
present business is, however, not with these last,
but with the negro creoles as they show themselves in the capital, where they muster five or
six to one among the entire population. Cheerful contentment is the prevailing expression of
every dusky face, whether turned towards you in
friendly morning greeting, as the busy swarm
presses on, talking, laughing, jesting, along the
highways to the market and quay, or in the
afternoon gatherings on the parade-ground,
under the avenues, and alongside of the river
banks. You watch and soon cease to wonder
that the official statistics of Paramaribo, while
enumerating and classifying its twenty-two
thousand inhabitants, make no distinctive headings of colour or race. I wish many other a
West Indian town could with equally good reason
permit themselves a like omission.

Glossy, however, as the surface may be, there
is a wrong side of the stuff, and to this we must
now turn our attention. Though a comfortable

and, so far at least as the majority of its in-
dwellers are concerned, a contented town, Paramaribo cannot, if compared, say, with Georgetown or Bridgetown, Kingston or even Port
d'Espagne, take rank as exactly prosperous or
progressive. True, the streets of the Creole
quarters of the city are constantly extending
themselves; there, new rows of small, neat dwellings, each with its gay garden and well-stocked
provision-ground, spring up year by year; but
in the commercial and what may, in a general
way, be termed the European quarter of the
town, large, half-empty stores, tall, neglected-
looking houses, a prevailing want of fresh repair
—here deficient paint, there broken woodwork—
besides a certain general air of listlessness, verging
on discouragement, and an evident insufficiency of
occupation, not from want of will, but of means,
all combine to give an appearance of stagnation suggestive of "better days," for the European colonists at least, in the past, and contrasting almost painfully with the more thriving back
streets and suburbs beyond. If any of my
readers have visited Italy in the sad, bygone
years when Italy was a geographical name only,

F

and there compared, as they may well have done, the trim "Borghi" of Grand-Ducal Florence with her stately but dilapidated Lungarno, or have, at Genoa, seen the contrast of those times between the palatial loneliness of Strada Balbi and the pretty, grove-embosomed villas of recent commercial date, they might, under all local differences of circumstance and colouring, recognize something not dissimilar, both in the meaning implied and effect produced, in this Transatlantic capital of Dutch Guiana.

The actual and immediate cause of decadence is a very common one, by no means peculiar to Paramaribo or Surinam—want of capital. Here, however, that want is, in a certain sense, doubled by the circumstance that not only are the means of the colony itself insufficient to its needs, but that there is no satisfactory prospect of an adequate supply from without. It is, I might almost say, the condition of a man indigent at home and friendless out of doors. The home-poverty is readily accounted for. It began with invasions, resistances, foreign occupations, treaty-embarrassments, and the other war-begotten ills of the troublous years that closed the last and

opened the present century. Followed next the
evil days already alluded to—evil for Trans-
atlantic colonies everywhere; and, in sequence
of the hostilities of 1833 between France and
Holland, doubly evil for Surinam. Then came
emancipation, long and unwisely deferred, till
financial exhaustion had reached its lowest
depths; and, with all these, the appalling con-
flagration of 1821, followed by one scarcely less
destructive in 1832; commercial difficulties of
every kind; the fatal yellow-fever epidemic of
1851,—in a word, a whole Pandora's box of
adversities, opened for Dutch Guiana in a scarcely
less disastrous profusion than for Jamaica herself.
And thus, to revert to the more special topic of
this chapter, Paramaribo was brought low indeed
—almost to the very gates of death; and her condition, as we this day see her, is that of a patient
recovering from a long and dangerous illness,
and weak, not indeed with the weakness of
actual disease, but the weakness of convalescence.

Nor is that convalescence likely to be a rapid
one. With Jamaica, we know, it has been otherwise; but then Jamaica is the child of a parent
alike vigorous and wealthy, able to chastise, able

also to assist. Not so with Dutch Guiana. In
more than one respect the good will of Holland
exceeds her power, and her comparatively recent
severance from Belgium, a political gain, was
yet a financial loss. Besides, Java is a more
popular name by far in the home mart of Dutch
enterprise than Surinam; and the Eastern colony
is indisputably the more attractive, the larger,
the wealthier, and, more, I believe, owing to external and accidental circumstances than to its
own intrinsic qualities as contrasted with those
of its rival, proportionally the more remunerative
of the two. Hence, while the invigorating
cordial, to continue our former metaphor, or,
rather, the true and certain panacea for the
patient's lingering ills, is poured out freely in the
direction of the Pacific, a feeble and interrupted
dribble is all that finds its way to the Atlantic
coast. Nor, again, can the annual subsidy with
which, for years past, the maternal Government
of the States has striven to uphold, and still up-
holds, the drooping vigour of her Western offspring, be regarded as a remedy adapted for the
case; it is, at best, a palliative, nor, I think—and
in this the wisest heads of the colony agree—one

conducive to genuine recovery and health. State
support, after this fashion, tends rather in its
results to cramp the energies of the recipient than
to develop them; it has something of the prop in
it, but more of the fetter. Compare, for example,
the French colonies, where it is most lavishly
bestowed, with the English, where the opposite
and almost niggardly extreme is the rule; the
conclusion is self-apparent, and the corollary, too.
Periodical subsidy, in particular, is an error—less
injurious, it may be, than the opposite conduct of
ungenerous Denmark, exacting for herself a yearly
tribute from her overtaxed and exhausted colonies,
but an error, nevertheless; it is the injudicious conduct of an over-indulgent parent, as the other is
that of a step-mother at best. Private enterprise, private capital, these are what Surinam
requires; and on the part of the mother country,
not a supplement to her coffers, but a guarantee.
Lastly, emancipation and its immediate and
inevitable consequences, the multiplication of
small freeholds, both of them events of yesterday
in Surinam, have not yet allowed time for the
balance of hired and independent labour to redress
itself; nor has the increase of creole well-being

yet reacted, as react it ultimately must, in a corresponding increase of prosperity among the European townsmen and estate-owners themselves. The present moment is one of transition, and transition implies that something has been left behind; a temporary loss even where more has been attained, or is in process of attainment.

While, seated in an upper balcony of Government House, we speculate on these things, the sun has set; twilight—at its very shortest in these latitudes—has brightened on into white moonlight; but the Militia town band, summoned by his Excellency to bear part in the hospitable entertainment of the evening, still gathers round it a motley and by no means silent crowd, assembled, some under the great tamarind-trees close by, and not a few within the Residential gardens themselves, thrown liberally open, on occasions like these, to public enjoyment.

CHAPTER III.

THE RIVER.

The river nobly foams and flows,
The charm of this enchanted ground ;
And all its thousand turns disclose
Some fresher beauty varying round.

BYRON.

WITH a subdued silvery gleam, the surest promise
in these latitudes of a clear day to follow, the
sun peeped through the network of the forest
that here does duty for horizon on every side,
when our party mustered under the neat wooden
pavilion of the landing-place, between the parade-
ground and the river,—I might have not less
correctly said the highway. For the true highways of this land are its rivers, traced right and
left with matchless profusion by Nature herself,
and more commodious could scarcely be found anywhere. Broad and deep, tidal, too, for miles up
their course, but with scarcely any variation in
the fulness of their mighty flow, summer or
winter, rainy season or dry, so constant is the

water-supply from its common origin, the equatorial mountain chain. They give easy access to
the innermost recesses of the vast regions beyond—
east, west, and south; and where their tortuous
windings and multiplied side-canals fail to reach,
Batavian industry and skill have made good the
want by canals, straighter in course, and often
hardly inferior in navigable capacity to the
mother rivers themselves. On the skeleton plan,
so to speak, of this mighty system of water communication the entire cultivation of the inland
has been naturally adjusted; and the estates of
Surinam are ranged one after another along the
margins of rivers and canals, just as farms might
be along highways and byways in Germany or
Hungary. Subservient to the water-ways, narrow
land-paths follow the river or trench, by which
not every estate alone, but its every subdivision
of an estate, every acre almost, is defined and
bordered, while the smaller dykes and canals are
again crossed by wooden bridges, maintained in
careful repair; but paths and bridges alike are of
a width and solidity adapted to footmen only, or
at best horsemen. The proper carriage road is
the river or canal.

In a climate like that of Surinam, bodily exertion is a thing to be economized as much as possible ; and accordingly everybody keeps his carriage—I beg pardon—his boat. That of the wealthy
estate-owner, of the vicarious " attorney " (not
a professional one, I may as well remark, for the
benefit of those unused to West Indian nomen-
clatures, but the holder of a power of attorney
on the proprietor's behalf), of the merchant, of
the higher official, and generally of every one
belonging to this or the other of what are conveniently called the " upper classes," is a comfortable barge, painted white for coolness' sake, and
propelled by oars varying in number from four
to eight. Towards the stern rises a deck cabin,
three, four, or even five curtained windows in
length, and capable of containing from six to ten
passengers at need, though more often occupied
only by the owner of the craft himself, stretched
out luxuriously at length, and secluded by closed
doors at either end of the apartment from the
toiling boatmen in front, and from the steersman,
who may be seen in the small space left open for
his duties at the stern of the vessel.

A fresh-painted, well-kept eight-oar, with a

cabin of the kind thus described, but of the very
largest dimensions, the sides, ceiling, hangings,
cushions, all white, with a dash of gilding here
and there; eight rowers dressed in loose white
suits, with broad red sashes round their waists,
and on their heads blue caps, to complete the
triple colours of the national flag, make a pretty
show on the sun-lit river. And the Governor's
barge might, for picturesque appearance, match
the caïque of a Stamboul dignitary, besides being
as much superior to the Eastern conveyance
in comfort as inferior in speed. The white-
painted six-oar, four-oar, or even two-oar barges,
too, that abound for ordinary voyaging, though,
of course, smaller in their dimensions and less
gay in their accessories, are pleasant objects to
look at, and may bring to mind the gondolas of
Venetian waters; with this difference, that
whereas the Adriatic crews are white, or what
should be white, and the boats black, here the
colours are, and not disadvantageously for pictorial effect, exactly reversed.

So much for the "genteeler sort." Larger
yet, and more solidly built, are the great lighter-
like barges, whether open or partly covered, that

convey down the stream, from the river-side estates,
casks of sugar or molasses, barrels of rum, sacks
of cocoa, heaped-up yams, plantains, sweet-
potatoes, cocoa-nuts, cassava, and the hundred
other well-known but too little cultivated products of this teeming land. Alongside of these
may be often seen the floating cottages of the
so-called "Bush negroes," well thatched and
snug, each occupying half or more of a wide
flat-bottomed boat, where two stalwart blacks in
genuine African garb—that is, next to no garb
(*vide* the woodcuts in Winwood Reade's amusing
narratives, *passim*)—paddle rather than row;
and any number of black ladies, hardly more
encumbered by their costume than their lords,
with an appropriate complement of ebony children, these last in no costume at all, look out
from the cabin-doors. In their wake follows a
raft of cut timber, green-heart, probably, or
brown-heart, or purple-heart, or balata, or letter-
wood, or locust-wood, or whatever other forest-
growth finds its market in town; and, standing
on it, one or more statuesque figures, that look
as if they had been cut out of dark porphyry by
no unskilful hand, and well polished afterwards,

guide its downward course. Most numerous of
all, light corials, that have retained the Indian
name as well as build, each one hollowed out of a
single tree-trunk, with sometimes a couple of
extra planks roughly tacked on to the sides by way
of bulwarks, paddle past, under the guidance of
one or two ragged negro labourers, or husband-
men, who exchange shouts, sometimes of jest,
sometimes of quarrel, with their fellows in other
boats or on the shore. These little skiffs, drawing
scarcely a foot of water when deepest laden, pass
through the narrowest ditches that divide almost
every acre of cultivated land on the estates from
the other, and are the chief means of passage for
the working-folks on their way to and fro between
country and town. When not in actual use, they
are kept sunk in water just deep enough to cover
them, and thus preserved from the sun-heat,
which would otherwise soon split the unseasoned
wood. Lastly, a few clumsy boats of the
ordinary long-shore type, in the service of trade
with the ships that lie anchored, giving out or
taking in cargo, off the town-wharf, mix up with
the rest, and add their quota of variety to the
river craft of Surinam.

However, on the present occasion, it is neither barge, plain or gay, nor a boat, nor even a corial, that is waiting to receive our party. A flat-bottomed river steamer, one of the three that belong to the service of the colony, lies off the wharf: she draws about ten feet of water, and her duty is just now to convey us up the Comme-weyne river, and its main tributary, the Cottica, where lies the district which his Excellency has selected for our inspection, because affording the greatest variety of scenery and cultivation within easy reach of Paramaribo. I have said that the colony possesses three of these boats; the largest of them makes a voyage along the sea-coast as far as Georgetown twice every month; the two smaller confine their excursions within the limits of river navigation.

In a few minutes we were all on board, a merry party, Dutch and English, official and non-official, military, naval, civilian, and burgher, but all of us bent alike on pleasing and being pleased, to the best of our opportunities. Our boat was well supplied, too, with whatever Dutch hospitality—no unsubstantial virtue—could furnish for convivial need, and was commanded by a

paragon of boat-captains, a bright-eyed, brown-
faced little man, Scotch by his father's side,
Indian by his mother's, himself uniting in
physiognomy, as in character, the shrewdness
and practical good sense of the former parentage
with the imperturbable calm and habitual good
humour of the latter. Under such auspices we
started on our way.

To enter the Commeweyne river we were first
obliged to retrace a portion of the route by which
I had arrived three days before, and to follow
the downward course of the Surinam river for
about eight miles, passing the same objects no
longer wholly new, but now more interesting
than before, because nearer seen and better understood. Here is a plantation, caught by glimpses
through the mangrove-scrub that borders the
river's bank; a narrow creek, at the mouth of
which several moored barges and half-submerged
corials are gathered, gives admittance to the
heart of the estate. It is a vast cocoa-grove,
where you may wander at will, under 350 continuous acres of green canopy; that is, if you are
ready to jump over any number of small brimming ditches, and to cross the wider irrigation-

trenches on bridges, the best of which is simply
a round and slippery tree trunk, excellently
adapted, no doubt, to the naked foot of a negro
labourer, but on which no European boot or shoe
can hope to maintain an instant's hold. Huge
pods, some yellow, some red,—the former colour
is, I am told, indicative of better quality,—
dangle in your face, and dispel the illusion by
which you might, at first sight of the growth and
foliage around you, have fancied yourself to be
in the midst of a remarkably fine alder-tree
thicket; while, from distance to distance, broad-
boughed trees, of the kind called by the negroes
" coffee-mamma," from the shelter they afford to
the plantations of that bush, spread their thick
shade high aloft and protect the cocoa-bushes and
their fruit from the direct action of the burning
sun. Moisture, warmth, and shade, these are the
primary and most essential conditions for the
well-doing of a cocoa estate. Innumerable
trenches, dug with mathematical exactitude of
alternate line and interspace, supply the first
requisite; a temperature that, in a wind-fenced
situation like this, bears a close resemblance for
humid warmth to that of an accurately shut hot-

house, assures the second; and the "coffee-mamma," a dense-leaved tree not unlike our own beech, guarantees the third. Thus favoured, a Surinam cocoa crop is pretty sure to be an abundant one. Ever and anon, where the green labyrinth is at its thickest, you come suddenly across a burly creole negro, busily engaged in plucking the large pods from the boughs with his left hand, while with a sharp cutlass held in his right he dextorously cuts off the upper part of the thick outer covering, and shakes the slimy agglomeration of seed and white burr clinging to it into a basket set close by him on the ground. A single labourer will in this fashion collect nearly 400 pounds weight of seeds in the course of a day. When full the baskets are carried off on the heads of the assistant field-women, or, if taken from the remoter parts of the plantation, are floated down in boats or corials to the brick-paved courtyard adjoining the planter's dwelling-house, where the nuts are cleansed and dried by simple and unexpensive processes, not unlike those in use for the coffee berry; after which nothing remains but to fill the sacks and send them off to their market across the seas.

A Guiana cocoa-plantation is an excellent investment. The first outlay is not heavy; nor is the maintenance of the plantation expensive, the number of labourers bearing an average proportion of one to nine to that of the acres under cultivation. The work required is of a kind that negroes, who are even now not unfrequently prejudiced by the memory of slave days against the cane-field and sugar-factory, undertake willingly enough; and, to judge by their stout limbs and evident good condition, they find it not unsuited to their capabilities. More than 4,000,000 pounds weight of cocoa are yearly produced in Surinam, " which is a consideration," as a negro remarked to me, laboriously attempting to put his ideas into English instead of the creole mixture of every known language that they use among themselves. Neither coolies nor Chinese are employed on these cocoa estates, much to the satisfaction of the creoles, who, though tolerant of, or rather clinging to, European mastership, have little sympathy with other coloured or semi-civilized races. Some authors have indeed conjectured that the West Indian labourer "of the future" will be a cross mixture of the African

G

and the Asiatic, but to this conclusion, desirable
or not, there is, for the present, no apparent
tendency either in Surinam or, to the best of my
knowledge, elsewhere. As to the Indians of
these regions, they keep to themselves; and their
incapacity of improvement, combined with hereditary laziness and acquired drunkenness, will, it
seems, soon render them a mere memory, poetical
or otherwise, of the past.

Soil, climate, and the conditions of labour, all
here combine to favour the cocoa-plant; and,
accordingly, out of the 30,000 acres actually
under cultivation in Dutch Guiana, we find that
a sixth part is dedicated to its production. More
would be, but for the time required before a fresh
plantation can bear a remunerative crop: five or six
years must, in fact, elapse, during which no return
at all is made, "which is a consideration" also,
though in an opposite sense to that quoted above.

Cocoa prospers; but, after all said and done,
sugar—the one thing that for two centuries and
more has been to the West Indies, Dutch,
French, Spanish, or English, what cloth is to
Manchester, cutlery to Sheffield, or beer to
Bavaria—is even now, despite of emancipation,

free-trade, beet-root, prohibitive regulations, American tariffs, and the whole array of adversities mustered against it for the last fifty years, the "favourite" of the agricultural race-course, and holds, with regard-to other products, however valuable, the same position as the queen of the chess-board does when compared with the remaining pieces. Indeed in some, Demerara for instance, sugar reigns, like Alexander Selkirk on his island, not only supreme, but alone; while in Surinam, where, more than in the generality of West Indian regions, she has many and, to a certain extent, successful rivals to contend with, she vindicates a full half of the reclaimed soil for her exclusive domain. Previous to emancipation, four-fifths at least were her allotted share. No fuller evidence of her former sway need be sought than that which is even yet everywhere supplied by the aspect of the great houses, gardens, and all the belongings of the old sugar plantations, once the wealth and mainstay of the Dutch colony. The garb is now too often, alas! "a world too wide for the shrunk shanks" of the present, but it witnesses to the time when it was cut to fitness and measure.

And here on our way, almost opposite the cocoa plantation with its modern and modest demesnes that we have just visited, appears the large sugar estate of Voorburg, close behind Fort Amsterdam, at the junction-point of the rivers. Let us land and glad the heart of the manager—the owner is, like too many others (and the more the pity), an absentee—by a visit. Happy indeed would he be, in his own estimation at least, were we to comply with his well-meant request of riding round every acre and inspecting every cane on the grounds. But as these cover 360 acres of actual cultivation, besides about a thousand more of yet unreclaimed concession, as the sun, too, is now high enough to be very hot, and we have other places to visit and sights to see, we will excuse ourselves as best we can, though by so doing we mark an indifference on our part to the beauties of the cane-field that he may forgive but cannot comprehend.

I may remark, by the way, that in this respect every planter, every manager, Dutch, English, Scotch, or Irish, in the West Indies is exactly the same. None of them, in the intense and per-

sonal interest they take in every furrow, every
cane, can understand how any one else can feel
less, or how, to the uninitiated eye, one acre of
reed is very like another, one ditch resembles
another ditch—just as the sheep in a flock are
mere repetitions, the one of the other, to all
but the shepherd, or as one baby resembles
any baby to every apprehension except to that
of the mother or, occasionally, the nurse. Let
us, however, respect what we are not worthy
to share; and do thou decline regretfully, O my
friend, but firmly—if thou desirest not headache
and twelve hours' subsequent stupefaction at the
least—the friendly invitation to "ride round"
the estates, in a sun-heat, say, of 140° Fahr., for
two whole hours—it cannot be less—while a super-
copious breakfast and all kinds of cheerful but
"seductive" drinks are awaiting thee on thy
return. Accompany us rather on the quiet circuit we now will make about the house, the
labourers' cottages, the outbuildings, and two,
at most three, acres of cane; and when in future
visiting on thy own account, "go and do like-
wise."

Nor is even the following picture of Voorburg

to be taken as a photographic likeness: rather an idealized view, combining details taken from other subjects with those of the above-named locality, and true to many—indeed most—sugar estates of this region, because limited to the exact facts, statistical or pictorial, of none.

Wood or brick—more often the former—the landing-place or "stelling" receives us, and on traversing it we are at once welcomed by the cool shelter—half a minute's exposure to the sun will have made you desire it—of a cool, well-swept, well-trimmed avenue, most often, as it happens to be at Voorburg itself, of mahogany-trees, dark and clustering, sometimes of light-green almond-trees or locust-trees, or it may be of palms, especially betel—this last selected rather for the perfect beauty of symmetry, in which it excels all other palms, than for shade. To this avenue, which may be from fifty to a hundred yards long, succeeds an open garden, laid out in walks, where "caddie" does duty for gravel, and flower-beds, in which roses, gera-niums, verbenas, jessamines, and other well-known Europeanized flowers and plants mix with their tropical rival, of equal or greater

beauty and sweetness; their names—ah, me! I
am no botanist—enough if wonderful passion-
flowers, noble scarlet lilies, and gorgeous cactus-
blossoms be mentioned here: Canon Kingsley's
chapter on the Botanical Gardens of Trinidad
may be safely consulted for the rest. Amid
these are a few flowering trees also — the
golden Pui (pronounced Poo'ee), the purple *Bois
immortel*, and the scarlet masses, entwined with
emerald-green, of the towering Spathodia, the
queen of the tropical forest. Among the beds and
garden-walks keep sentinel, in true Batavian
fashion, quaint, white-painted wooden statues,
mostly classical, after Lemprière, "all heathen
goddesses most rare"—Venuses, Dianas, Apollos,
Terpsichores, Fortunes on wheels, Bacchuses,
Fauns, occasionally a William, a Van Tromp,
or some other hero of Dutch land or main—
these last recognizable by the vestiges of cocked
hats and tail-coats, as the former by the absence
of those or any other articles of raiment, and all
with their due proportion of mutilated noses,
lopped hands, and the many injuries of sun, rain,
and envious time.

But stay, I had almost forgot to mention the

two iron popguns that command the landing-
place, and flank on either side the entry of the
avenue—imitation cannon, that, in everything,
except their greater size, are the very counter-
parts of those " devilish engines " that our early
childhood thought it a great achievement to load
and fire off. Here the children's part is played
not unsuccessfully by the negroes themselves,
who, at seventy years of age, have no less pleasure than we ourselves might have felt at seven,
in banging off their artillery in and out of all
possible seasons, but especially on the approach
of distinguished and popular visitors like ourselves; I mean, of course, his Excellency the
Governor, with whom I am happily identified,
so to speak, during this trip. But this is not all;
for within the garden, close under the house-
windows, are ranged two, four, or even six more
pieces, some shaped like cannon, others like
mortars; and these too are crammed up to their
very mouths with powder and improvized wad-
ding, and exploded on festive occasions, when,
as ill hap will have it, their over-repletion often
results in bursting, and their bursting in the
extemporized amputation of some negro arm,

leg, or head, as the case may be. But, though
I heard of many a heart-rending or limb-rending
event of the kind, I am thankful to say that
I witnessed none during our tour, though of
explosions many.

Next a flight of steps, stone or brick, guarded
by a handsome parapet in the Dutch style, and
surmounted by a platform, with more or less of
architectural pretension, leads up to the wide
front door, by which we pass, and find ourselves
at once in the large entrance-hall, that here, as
formerly in European dwellings, serves for
dining-room and reception-room generally. The
solid furniture, of wood dark with age, gives it a
quasi old-English look, and the gloom—for the
light is allowed but a scanty entrance, lest her
sister, heat, should enter too—is *quasi* English also.
But the stiff portraits on the wall, ancestors,
relatives, Netherland celebrities, royal person-
ages, governors, &c., &c., are entirely Dutch,
and belong to the " wooden " school of art. The
central table is of any given size and strength,
and has been evidently calculated for any amount
of guests and viands. We shall partake of the
latter before leaving, and bestow well-merited

praise on cook and cellar. Besides the hall are
other apartments, counting-rooms, and so forth;
above it is a second story; above it a third; for
the brick walls are strong, and hurricanes are
here, as in Demerara, by Miss Martineau's leave,
unknown; over all rises a high-pitched roof;
the wolf, or griffin, or lion, or whatever crest the
original proprietor may have boasted, figures
atop as gable ornament or vane. The whole
forms a manor-house that might have been trans-
ported, by substantial Dutch cherubs of course,
as the Loretto bauble was by slim Italian an-
giolets, from amid the poplars of Arnheim or
Bredevoort, and set down on the banks of
Commeweyne. Only the not unfrequent adjuncts
of a trellised verandah and a cool outside
gallery are manifestly not of extra-tropical
growth.

We have received our welcome, and drunk
our prelusory " schnapps." And now for the
sight-seeing. The factory, where the canes are
crushed into mere fibre, as fast as the negroes
can lift them from the canal-barge alongside on
to the insatiable rollers close by, give out their
continuous green frothy stream, to be clarified,

heated, boiled, reboiled, tormented fifty ways, till it finds refuge in the hogsheads or rum-barrels, resembling in every stage of its course its counterpart in Demerara, or Jamaica, minus however, except in one solitary instance, the expensive refinements of the centrifugal cylinder and vacuum pan. But for mere delectation, unless heat, vapour, noise, and an annihilation of everything in general to a sugar thought in a sugar shade— forgive me, Marvell!—be delectation, which I hardly think, no man need linger in a factory, nor, unless he desires premature intoxication on vapour, in a rum-distillery either. Worth attention, however, and admiration too, is the solidity of construction by which the huge mass of building, doubly heavy from the ponderous machinery it contains, besides its clustering group of out-houses, megass-sheds, tall chimneys, store-places, and the rest, is enabled to support itself upright and unyielding on a soil so marshy and unstable. The foundations in many instances, I am told, exceed by double in surface - dimension the buildings above.

Ingenious bees, these sugar-making ones. Let us next look at the hives of the workers. These

workers, or, metaphor apart, labourers, are here
—at Voorburg, I mean—and on not a few other
estates, of three kinds, coolie, Chinese, and
creole. And should any one, smitten with a
desire for accuracy and statistics, wish to know
their exact numbers in this particular instance,
the coolies at Voorburg are ninety all told,
the Chinese 181, the creoles or colonial-born
negroes, 200.

First to the coolies. Their introduction into
Surinam is of recent date—little over two
years, in fact; but everything has been organized for them on exactly the same footing
as in Demerara or Trinidad. They have
their agents, here and in India their official
protector—a very efficient one, in the person of
Mr. A. C——, her Majesty's Consul. Their
labour and pay regulations are textually identical
with those of Demerara. They are duly provided with a medical staff and hospitals; in a
word, they are, if anything, more fenced in here
from every shadow of a grievance than even in
an English colony: Mr. Jenkins himself could
not ask more for his *protégés*. The eye recog-
nizes at once the regulation cottages, all, like

pretty maids—but here the similarity ceases—of
a row, with garden spaces attached, back yards,
verandahs, and every attention paid by the con-
structors to dryness, ventilation, and whatever
else a Parliamentary Inspector of the most
practical type could desire. Thus much is done
for the immigrants; but except to amass money,
with an occasional whiff at the hooka between
times, from morning to night, the "mild
Hindoo" is not inclined to do much for himself.
His garden, ill planted, and ill cared for, is a
sorry sight; his dwelling, for what concerns the
interior, is a cross between a gipsy hut and a rag-
shop, and a pinched, stingy meanness characterizes his every belonging, no less than himself.
That he may also excel in "grace, ease,
courtesy, self-restraint, dignity, sweetness, and
light" I am ready, of course, with all believers
in "At last," to admit. But I do it on faith,
"the evidence of things not seen," either in the
West Indies or the East. Low-caste Hindoos in
their own land are, to all ordinary apprehension,
slovenly, dirty, ungraceful, generally unaccept-
able in person and surroundings; and the coolies
of Voorburg may have been low caste, very

likely. Yet, offensive as is the low-caste Indian, were I estate-owner or colonial governor, I had rather see the lowest Parias of the low than a single trim, smooth-faced, smooth-wayed, clever, high-caste Hindoo on my lands or in my colony.

But for the untidiness, I might say shiftlessness, of the Surinam-planted coolies some allowance must be made. They are new-comers in a new land, among what are to them new races; and if it takes some time even for the European under such like circumstances to pluck up heart and be a-doing, the process of adaptation is yet slower for the Asiatic. In Demerara, where they have now dwelt for years, with Europeans to stimulate and direct them, and negroes to teach them gardening without doors and tidiness within, the coolies certainly make a better show, and so do their dwellings. But they have much as yet to learn in Surinam.

Passing a dyke or two, we come next on the Chinese cottages, in construction and outward arrangement identical with those of the coolies, or nearly so. The gardens here show a decided improvement, not indeed in the shape of flowers, or of any of the pretty, graceful things of the

soil, for of such are none here, but in
useful vegetables and pot-herbs in plenty.
Spade and hoe, manure and water, care and
forethought, have done their work, and are
receiving their reward. But, the inside of a
Chinese dwelling; "*guarda e passa.*" Well,
Chinamen are fond of pigs; and if they have a
fancy themselves to live in pigsties, it is all in
character.

A dyke or two more has to be crossed, and we
enter the Creole village. Here regulation has
done less, and individual will and fancy more.
But the negroes are Dutch trained, and have an
idea of straight lines and orderly rows by no
means African; though in the English-like preference given to isolated dwellings, in which each
household can live apart, over conjoint ones, they
do but follow the custom of their ancestral birthplace. Their gardens are well stocked, not with
fruit and vegetables only, with plantains, mangoes,
bananas, yams, sweet potatoes, peas, and such
like things good for food, but also with whatever
is pleasant to the eye; with gay flowers, twining
creepers, bright berries, scarlet and black; in
fine, with the brilliant colours and strong con-

trasts that befit African taste. Inside their
dwellings are comfortable, and in most instances
clean, neatly arranged too, though the space is
very often overcrowded with furniture, the tables
covered with cheap glass and crockery, more for
show than use, and the walls hung round with a
confused medley of gaudy prints. These creoles
evidently know how to enjoy life, and have
resolved to make the best of it—the wisest
resolution, it may be, for us mortals in our little
day.

Enough of creoles, Chinese, and coolies for
this once; we are yet at the outset of our voyage.
Returning towards the factory, we pay a visit to
the airy and well-constructed hospital. Sore feet,
the result of neglected chigoes, seem the principal
complaint. For the climate is, in itself, a healthy
one; epidemics are rare, marsh fever scarcely
heard of, and yellow-fever, like cholera, a historical event of years past. Hence disease, when
it occurs, is mostly traceable to some distinct
cause of individual folly, unreasonable custom,
or, as is frequently the case with the self-stinting
coolie, insufficient diet. Nor is there any doubt that
here, as in almost every other West Indian colony

—Demerara is one of the few honourable exceptions—sanitary regulations and medical service
are far from their best. Let them be reformed,
as they easily may, and the inhabitant, European
or other, of the Guiana coast, will have no reason
to complain of his lot, so far as climate is concerned, even when contrasted with the bracing
atmosphere and invigorating breezes of the
northern sea-shore.

A look at the truly regal king-palm, an African
importation, and said to be the only specimen in
the colony, that waves its crown of dense fronds,
each thirty and forty feet long, in front of the
Voorburg Residence, and we re-embark; not
sorry, after the hot sunshine we have endured, to
find ourselves once more under the boat-awning
in the temperate river breeze.

In a few minutes more we have rounded the
point of Fort Amsterdam, where of course flags
are flying, and officers and soldiers, in all the
glory of uniform, are hastily marshalling themselves alongside of the battery at the water's
edge, to greet his Excellency, who, hat in hand,
acknowledges their salutations from the deck.
And now, with the tide to help, we are steaming

H

up the giant Commeweyne, and enter straight
on a scene of singular beauty, and a character
all its own. For breadth of stream, indeed, and
colour, or discolour, of water, the river hereabouts—that is, for about twenty miles of its
lower course—might fairly pass for the Danube
anywhere between Orsova and Widdin, or perhaps for a main branch of the Nile above Benha,
with the sole discrepancy that whereas the Commeweyne, thanks to the neighbouring Atlantic,
is tidal, the two last-named tributaries of the
tideless Mediterranean and Black Seas are not
so. But that large, reddish water-snake, that
writhes its ugly way up the current, that timber-
raft of rough-hewn but costly materials, bearing
on its planks the tall, naked African figures that
guide its way; that light Indian corial, balanced
as venturesomely as any Oxford skiff, and
managed by a boatman as skilful, however
ragged his clothes and reckless his seeming, as
the precisest Oxford undergraduate; that gleam-
ing, gondola-like barge, with its covered cabin—
is the reclining form within dark or fair?—and
its cheery, singing crew,—all these are objects
not of Bulgarian nor even, though not absolutely

dissimilar, of Egyptian river-life. The hot light
mirrored on the turbid water, the moist, hot
breeze, the intense, hot stillness of earth and sky
between which the very river seems as if motion-
less and sleeping in the monotony of its tepid
flow,—these also are unknown to the Nile of the
Cairene Delta or the Turko-Wallachian Danube;
they belong to a more central zone. Details of
the sort might, however, be every one of them—
the "Bush negroes" and the covered Dutch
barges excepted—equally well found, as I myself
can bear witness, on the Essequibo, the Demerara,
or any other of the neighbouring Guiana coast
rivers. But not so the scarcely interrupted succession of estates, sugar, cocoa, and plantain, to the
right and left, each with its quaint name, most
often Dutch, telling some tale of the hopes, cares,
expectations, anxieties, affections, joys, sorrows,
of former owners long ago. Thus the mental
phases of a John, a Peter, an Anna, an Eliza-
beth, are each duly commemorated in the names
of "Pieterszorg," "Johannishoop," "Anna's
Lust," and "Elizabeth-hoop"; self-confidence
speaks in "Vlugt-en-Trow" ("Duty and Trust");
philosophy, practical at any rate, in "Rust-en-

Werk " (" Rest and Labour "). The happy owners of "Pleasure and Rest," "Peace," "Union," "Gratitude," and "Satisfaction" ("Lust tot Rust," "Vriede," "Eendracht," "Dankbaarheid," and "Lustrijk") deserved, we may hope, the congratulations they still seem to claim; while "Incomplete," with "Profit and Loss" ("Nuit Volmacht," "Nuit en Schadelijk"), leave us in doubt. Gloomier yet, "Labour and Sorrow," "Discord," and, worst of all, "Envy and Spite" ("Moed en Kommer," "Discordia," "Nijd en Spijt ") remain as recollections of recollections long since faded, a sorry score long since, we may reasonably trust, wiped out, and, but for these now unmeaning names, forgotten. Good deeds and pleasurable things have short-lived memories, it is true; but sorrows and wrongs have, in the majority of instances, shorter still.

Various as were, to judge by the catalogue of which I have just given a random sample, the early fortunes of the "Estates," their later times have been to the full as varied, or, perhaps, more. Some have, by good management, backed with the requisite capital, retained through all vicissitudes of trade and strife, of slavery, apprentice-

ship, and emancipation, a sufficiency of creole
labour to retain all, or the greater part of their
old West-Indian prosperity, and announce themselves accordingly, as we sail past, by smoking
chimneys, roofs and walls in good repair, and
clustering cottages, amid the dense green of cocoa
groves, or the verdant monotony of sugar-canes,
only interrupted at regular distances by canal and
dyke, or by some long palm row, planted more
for beauty than for profit, a huge cotton-tree,
magnificent to look at, but useless else, and chiefly
spared to humour negro superstition, that yet
brings offerings of food and drink to the invisible
power, rather maleficent than otherwise, supposed to reside under its boughs. Or, again,
signs of recent additions and improvements, with
long white rows of regulation-built cottages, the
tenements of coolies or Chinese, attest fortunes,
not only maintained, but improved, by the in-
fusion of "new blood" from the Indian or the
Celestial Empire. Or a reverse process has taken
place : the cane has abdicated in favour of less
costly, but also less remunerative, rivals; and
the white proprietor has made place for a black
land-owner, or, more commonly, for several, who

now cultivate the land in accordance with their
narrow means. Here the emerald monotony of
the land is broken; patches of cassava-growth,
like an infinity of soft green cupolas crowded one
on the other, and undulating to every breath of
air, show chequerwise between acres where the metallic glitter of vigorous plantain leaves or tall, hop-
like rows of climbing yam tell of an unexhausted
and seemingly inexhaustible soil. Jotted freely
amid the lesser growths, fruit-trees of every kind
spread unpruned with a luxuriance that says more
for the quantity than the quality of their crop;
but this is the tropical rule, and even Dutch
gardening skill is unavailing against the exube-
rance of growth in climates like these. Meanwhile, the stately residence of the former proprietor—who, by the way, had, in all probability,
been for many years an absentee, before, by a
natural result, he became a bankrupt (the transition is a stereotyped one, and recurs every day)—
has at last been totally abandoned as out of keeping with the simpler requirements of Cudjoe and
his fellows, who content themselves with small
cottages half buried in a medley of flower-bushes
and kitchen-growth close by; though in more

than one instance our dusky creole, reverting to
the hereditary Oriental instinct of ease and how to
take it, has built himself, on the green margin of
some creek or river inlet, a pretty painted kiosk,
worthy of finding place among its likenesses on
the shores of the Bosphorus or Nile, and answer-
ing the same ends. An unroofed factory and
ruined chimney close by combine to mark the
present phase, a necessary though a transient one,
of land-ownership, through which Surinam is
passing, a more hopeful one, though less brilliant,
than that of exclusively large estates and costly
factories owned by few.

As the river shores, so is the country behind,
for miles away on either side, a chequer-board
of field and plantation, intersected by straight
ditches and canals, sluices, water-gates, locks, and
dams, with an occasional patch of unreclaimed
bush or towering forest, and studded with little
cottage clusters, where any quantity of negro
children play in the dust before the doors, and
curs innumerable lie in wait to rush out and yelp
at the passing stranger.

The ditches are crossed, at frequent intervals,
by wooden bridges, and over these run well-kept

horse-paths, that skirt the canals, and go from estate to estate through the entire district. Often, too, they pass under noble avenues of locust or mahogany-trees, or between tall palm rows, where the turf on either side allows a pleasant canter off the beaten track. Friendly greetings from labourer and peasant meet me everywhere " as I ride, as I ride," and salutations, not so gracefully subservient, perhaps, as those of the Hindoo, but much more cheerful and sincere.

I am again,—for this is not a diary where everything is put down according to the order in which it occurred, but rather a landscape picture, where I take the liberty of arranging accessories as best may suit convenience or effect,—I am again on board our steamer, onward bound with the rest. Sometimes our course lies along the centre of the river, and then we have a general view of either side, far off, but seen in that calmness of atmosphere unknown to the northern climes, which, while it abolishes the effects of distance, creates a curious illusion, making the smallness of the remoter objects appear, not relative, but absolute. Sharp-edged and bright-coloured in the sun, houses and cottages stand out in an apparent

foreground of tree and field ; miniature dwellings
among a miniature vegetation, with Lilliputian
likenesses of men and women between. Then
again we approach one or the other bank, and
see! the little palm-model is sixty feet high at
least, and the gabled toy-house a large mansion
three or four stories high. And now the fields
and gardens reach down to the very brink of the
stream, and our approach has been watched by
the labourers from far ; so that, by the time we
are gliding alongside, troops of blacks, men and
women,—the former having hastily slipped on
their white shirts, the latter re-arranged
their picturesque headkerchiefs, of every device
and colour, gala fashion,—hurry down to the
landing-place for a welcome. Some bear with
them little Dutch or fancy flags ; others, the
children especially, have wild-flowers in their
hands : two or three instruments of music, or
what does duty for such, are heard in the crowd ;
and a dense group forms, with the eager serious-
ness befitting the occasion, about the two dwarf
cannon by the wharf-side, which are now banged
off amid the triumphant shouts of the one sex
and the screams of the other. We, on the deck

and paddle-boxes, return the greetings as best we may; the Governor waves his hat, fresh shouts follow, till the popular excitement, on shore be it understood, takes the form of a dance, begun for our delectation, and continued for that of the dancers themselves long after we have glided away. White dresses, dashed here and there by a sprinkling of gay colours; behind them a glowing screen of garden flowers, further back and all around the emerald green of cane-fields; overhead tall palms, not half seared and scant of foliage, as we too frequently see them in the wind-swept islands of the Caribbean Archipelago, but luxuriant with their heavy crowns, or giant flowering trees, crimson and yellow, the whole flooded, penetrated everywhere, by the steady brightness of the tropical day—

> "Till all things seem only one
> In the universal sun,"—

a gay sight, and harmonizing well with the sounds of welcome, happiness, and mirth. These tell, not indeed perhaps of all-absorbing industry, of ventursome speculation, and colossal success, but of sufficiency, contentment, and well-doing— good things too in their way.

Salutations duly acknowledged—this may be the tenth estate where the ceremony has been repeated, during about a decade of miles up the river,—we retreat under the cool of the awning for quiet talk; and now the brown-complexioned, bright-eyed, demure little semi-Indian captain, courteously coming up, suggests a glass of Hollands, tempered with grateful ingredients, and prepared in one or other of the many ways known to West Indian convivality. The proposal meets with universal acceptance, and we all join in pledging the health and happiness of the colony of Surinam, and of its excellent and deservedly popular Governor.

CHAPTER IV.

COTTICA.

—A leaf on the one great tree, that, up from old time
Growing, contains in itself the whole of the virtue and life of
Bygone days, drawing now to itself all kindreds and nations,
And must have for itself the whole world for its root and
   branches.
                                                CLOUGH.

POPULARITY is rarely denied to merit; but, for one
cause or another, it is sometimes deferred till it
takes the form of a post-mortem tribute. And
thus it has fared with Cornelis van Aersson, more
generally known by his territorial style of Sommelsdyk, who erected the fort now in view as we
approach the junction of the Commeweyne and
Cottica rivers. Van Sommelsdyk, who, in the
month of November, 1683, arrived to govern the
Guiana territory, a third part of which he already
owned as proprietor, had been a page in the
Court of William II., of Orange, an intimate
friend of our own William III., and had held
such high office in his own country as befitted his

noble and ancient birth and great administrative talents. To these advantages he added, if his portraits be correct, a more than ordinary beauty of feature and great dignity of bearing.

The colony, when Van Sommelsdyk took charge of it, was in a wretched state, disorganized, or rather never yet properly organized at all within, and harassed by continual attacks on the part of the native Indians, then formidable by their numbers, from without. To repress these, and thus secure the leisure necessary for internal reforms, was the new Governor's first object; and with such vigour and skill did he address himself to the task, that within a year's time the Indians, repulsed on every side, were glad to ask for peace. It was granted them on equitable terms, and the principal tribes, Caribs, Warrows, and Arrowoks, received the rights of freedom and land; henceforth no longer enemies, but fellow-citizens and allies. This done, Van Sommelsdyk hastened to extend the now-unharassed frontier by founding, in the second year of his rule, with the co-operation of Samuel Cohen Nassy—a modern Joshua in Israel—the important Hebrew settlement, far up the valley of the Surinam river, afterwards known as the "Joden Savannah," or Jews' Savannah, and which, during the following century, was, for quality and extent of cultivation, the wealthiest district of Dutch Guiana. Less noted at the time, but more important in its results, because more lasting, was the benefit he conferred on the colony at large by the cocoa-plant, first brought by his foresight into cultivation the following year.

It was, however, by the repression of crime and the enforcement of law and order among the colonists themselves, and especially among the garrison soldiers, whose undisciplined conduct and frequent excesses had rendered them hitherto the standing disgrace and terror of the settlement, that he established his best claim to the gratitude of his subjects, bond or free. The soldiers, no longer indulged in the idleness of garrison quarters, were kept constantly occupied on expeditions of war or discovery inland, or employed in digging the great canal that, starting from Paramaribo, joins the Surinam to the Saramacca, and still bears the name of Sommelsdyk; while others constructed the two forts, one of which is now before us on the Commeweyne, the

other stands at the junction of the Para and
Surinam rivers. At the same time a High Court
of Justice, the first known in the colony, was, by
his care, erected, before which offenders of all
descriptions, and not rarely masters guilty of
cruelty to their slaves, were brought for sentence;
and the Governor himself, by public proclama-
tion three times renewed, announced himself
amenable, like any other individual in the colony,
to legal summons and jurisdiction, disclaiming
the protection of any personal privilege soever,
and declaring his readiness to make any repara-
tion, should the sentence of the court require it.

For since, as Van Sommelsdyk had officially
declared in a dispatch dated the 16th January,
1684, " the misfortunes of the colony had been
mainly due to the unworthy conduct of its
Governors, who had only sought their own profit
to the ruin of the common weal," he rightly
thought that the example of better things should
first be set by himself as Governor and head.
This, for the five years of his administration, he
did nobly and steadily. Meanwhile the colony, as
was natural under such a rule, grew and prospered,
till its limits, formerly restricted to the immediate

neighbourhood of Paramaribo, included the courses of the great rivers, Saramacca and Commeweyne, west and east; while up the Surinam itself they reached to a distance of sixty miles or more from the coast; and the total number of estates, only fifty at the time of Van Sommelsdyk's arrival, had increased to two full hundred.

But while Van Sommelsdyk, by his energetic integrity, earned the thanks and admiration of the colony at large, he drew down on himself, by a necessary consequence, the bitter hatred of those who had been accustomed to find their advantage or gratify their passions under a different system of administration, and, foremost among such, of the soldiery, who chafed under a discipline alike needful and severe. A mutiny that broke out on the 17th July, 1688, soon became general; and the Governor, hastening to quell it in person, fell its first victim, pierced with six-and-forty wounds, inflicted by the mutineers, who at the same time murdered the commander of the garrison, and took possession of the fort and town, which for four days endured all the horrors of military anarchy. But the spirit of

the late Governor had passed into the magistracy
he had created; and in a few days order was
re-established, and confirmed by the execution of
eleven of the ringleaders and the expulsion of
the rest. Van Sommelsdyk's grave was dug near
the orange-grove where he died, close by the
walls of the fort : but his work remained ; and on
the foundations of order and discipline, cemented
by his blood, the colony reared its after-super-
structure of lasting prosperity. His son, Francis
van Aerssen, Lord of Chatillon, declined, at his
mother's prayer, the offered Governorship of the
colony ; but accompanied the newly appointed
Governor thither in a private capacity next year,
and upheld the family reputation by the courage
and skill with which he headed the repulse of a
piratical attempt made by the French, who, with
nine men-of-war and a whole flotilla of gun-boats,
commanded by Admiral De Casse, attempted to
profit by the temporary confusion of Dutch affairs.
Under the joint leadership of Francis of Chatillon
and the gallant Hebrew chief, Nassy, mentioned
before, the colonists obtained a complete victory
over their invaders, and for several years after
enjoyed the advantages of peace abroad and

I

good government at home, won for them by Van
Sommelsdyk and his son. The States of Holland
and William the Third of England testified by
their conduct towards the widowed mother the
respect felt for the memory of the great Surinam
Governor in his native land.

During the whole of the eighteenth century,
Fort Sommelsdyk continued to be a position of
the greatest importance, covering the bulk of the
colonial estates and the capital itself from the
frequent inroads of Cayenne depredators, and
their allies, the French maroons. With the final
repression of these marauders, the military duties
of the post may be said to have ceased; and
it has now for several years served only as a
police-station. No spot could have been better
chosen; no truer centre found anywhere. Not
only does the Commeweyne river, with its double
fringe of estates and cultivation reaching far to
the south, here unite with its main tributary, the
Cottica, the eastern artery of a wide and populous
district, but the same way gives direct access to
the Perica river, another important affluent from
the south-east; while at a little distance the Matap-
pica watercourse branches off in a northerly

direction, and, winding amid a populous region of plantations and cane-fields, finds an opening to the sea beyond. Half the cultivation and, owing to the character of the estates, more than half the rural population of Dutch Guiana are within the range of these districts; and the selection of this post will ever remain a proof of the administrative no less than of the military talents of Van Sommelsdyk.

The small fort, a pentagon, erected on a grass-grown promontory at the meeting of the two great waters, has a very pretty appearance. On every side the further view is shut off by the dense forest, through which the rivers make their winding way by channels from thirty to forty feet in depth; no other habitation is in sight; and the cleared space around the fort buildings has an out-of-the-world look, befitting a scene of weird-adventure in "Mabensgion" or the "Fairie Queene." But the poetry of the New World is in itself, not in the eyes of those who behold it; and if fairies exist west of the Atlantic, they are invisible the most. Above its junction, the Commeweyne changes character, and, instead of being a broad slow-flowing volume of brackish water, becomes a comparatively narrow but deep and rapid stream; while its former muddy colour is exchanged for pure black, not unlike the appearance of the mid-Atlantic depths in its inky glassiness. If taken up, however, in small quantity, the black colour, which is due chiefly to the depth, gives place to a light yellow ; otherwise the water is clear, free from any admixture of mud, and perfectly healthy, with a slightly astringent taste. These peculiarities are popularly ascribed to some vegetable extract of the nature of tannin, derived from the decomposing substances of the equatorial forest underneath which these rivers take their rise.

We, for our part, no longer pursue our voyage on the Commeweyne, but diverging follow its tributary, or, rather, equal stream, the Cottica, and our course is henceforth east, almost parallel with the sea line, though at some distance from it. From Fort Sommelsdyk onwards the view on either bank gains in beauty what it loses in extent. The bendings and turnings of the river are innumerable ; indeed it not rarely coils on itself in an almost circular loop, the nearest points of which have been in many instances

artificially connected by a short but deep and
navigable canal, the work of Dutch industry.
Several little islands, each an impenetrable
mass of tangled vegetation, have thus been
formed; on two larger ones, far up the river,
coffee is still grown. It was for many years one
of the main articles of cultivation in these
districts, though now it has fallen into unmerited
neglect; whence it will doubtless be rescued
whenever a better-proportioned labour supply
shall allow the colonist to re-occupy and extend
the narrow limits within which their activity
is at present restricted. Several creeks, as all
lesser watercourses are here called, fall into the
main stream, or from distance to distance connect
it by the aid of canals with the sea. On the
banks of one of these flourished in days gone by
the still-famous Helena, a mulatto syren, whose
dusky charms are said to have rivalled in their
mischievous effects, if not in other respects, those
of her Grecian namesake. These creeks, with
the canals and ditches dependent on them, complete the water system, alike of irrigation and
traffic, throughout this wonderful land, where
nature has done so much and art and skill yet

more. But, whatever the sea-communication through these occasional openings, no brackish taint ever finds its way to the higher level through which the Cottica flows; and the freshness of the water is betokened by the ever-increasing loveliness and variety of the river-side vegetation. Lowest down hangs the broad fringe of the large-leaved "moco-moco," a plant that has, I suppose, some authentic Latin name, only I know it not; nor would it, however appropriate, give thee, perhaps, gentle reader, any clearer idea of the plant than may its Indian one, dipping its glossy green clusters into the very stream. Above tower all the giants of West Indian and South American forests, knit together by endless meshes of convolvulus, liane, creeper, and wild vine,—the woorali, I am told, among the rest; and surcharged with parasitic orchises, till the burden of a single tree seems sufficient to replenish all the hot-houses of England and Wales from stove to roof. Piercing through these, the Eta palm—it resembles in growth the toddy palm of the East Indies, and, for aught my ignorance can object to the contrary, may be the very same—waves its graceful fans high against the steady

blue; and birds innumerable, black, white,
mottled, plain, blue, yellow, crimson, long-billed,
parrot-billed, a whole aviary let loose, fly among
the boughs, or strut fearless between the tree-
trunks, or stand mid-leg deep meditative in the
water. Large lizards abound on the banks; and
snakes too, it may be, but they have the grace to
keep out of sight, along with the jaguars and
other unpleasant occupants of the Guiana jungle.
In their stead light corials, sometimes with only
a woman to paddle, sometimes a man or boy,
dart out of the harbour-like shelter of the creeks;
Bush-negro families peer curiously from the doors
of their floating cottages, or guide their timber-
rafts down the stream. Ever and anon a white
painted barge, conveying an overseer, a book-
keeper, or some other of the white or semi-white
gentry, rows quickly by; for the river is the highway, and the wayfarers along it many; so that
even where its banks are at the loneliest, the
stream itself has life and activity enough to show.
More often, however, it passes between cultivated
lands; for while the factories and sugar estates
diminish in number as we go further up, the
small Creole properties increase, and comfortable

little dwellings, places, cottages, sheds, and out-
houses, amid every variety of "provision-ground"
cultivation, multiply along the bank.

Here, too, even more than along the Commeweyne, men in every variety of costume, from
the raggedest half-nakedness that in this climate
betokens not exactly want, but rather hard out-
door work, to the white trousers and black coat,
the badges of the upper-class negro creole, and a
yet greater number of women, who have fortunately not learned to exchange the becoming
and practical turban of their race for the ridiculous
hat and bonnet of European fashion, come down
to honour the Governor's passage; nor does the
blazing afternoon sun, now at his hottest, seem to
have the least effect on the energy of their
welcome. And I may add that not here only,
and in the more secluded districts of the colony,
but throughout its entire extent I neither saw
nor heard of anything indicating, however
remotely, the duality of feeling that in so
many other West Indian settlements — the
Danish most—draws a line of separation, if not
hostility, between the black and the white
inhabitants of the land. The creoles of Surinam

are not less loyal to the Dutch tricolor than the burghers of Leyden, and King William himself could hardly expect a more affectionately enthusiastic greeting, were he to make a tour through the Seven Provinces, than his representative receives when visiting his Transatlantic subjects of the same rule. And, in this matter, observation is confirmed by history ; nor, since the conclusion, in 1777, of the long and bloody maroon wars, has a single outbreak or show of insubordination disturbed the interior harmony of Dutch Guiana.

For this happy state of things, contrasting so advantageously with the records of too many other neighbouring colonies, the wise and kindly rule of an enlightened Government has been, of course, the principal promoter and cause. But no small share of the praise is also due to the truest friends and best guides Europe has ever supplied to the African race—the Moravian Brothers.

That Christianity was in the " good old times," a century back, never taught to slaves, that its introduction among them was vehemently opposed, if not positively prohibited by actual law, or

custom stronger than law itself, may nowadays
shock, but should not surprise us. Slavery is in
itself too absolute an inequality, too marked an
injustice of man towards man, to allow of com-
munity, that is, of an association on equal terms
in other respects, least of all in religion. And so
long as slavery was intended to be perpetual, it
was necessary that the distinctions behind which
it entrenched itself should be perpetual also. It
might be objected that in matters professedly
regarding the other world such severe demarcation was less necessary than in the more tangible
condition of this ; but a little attention will show
the opposite to be the fact. What is incapable of
proof is also incapable of refutation ; a boundary
line that cannot be defined cannot be disputed;
and dogmatic or so-called spiritual distinctions,
however indefensible by right reason, have also
the more than counterbalancing advantage of
being inassailable from the same quarter. They
are like the assertion, should any one choose to
make it, that Mars or Venus are inferior planets to
our own, because Mars, forsooth, is inhabited by
bears, and Venus by monkeys. Nation after nation,
following this happy line of argument, has boldly

denied the common rights of this world to rivals
or strangers, on the plea that the rights of another
world were not theirs. Examples would be
invidious; they will readily occur to every mind
conversant, even superficially, with history, profane or other. Nor, indeed, does that "foulest
birth of time," sectarian persecution, rest on any
other basis; though here it is not a mere pretext,
but a direct cause. And thus it follows conversely
that intercommunity of religion, from whichever
side, upper or lower, conqueror or conquered,
ruler or ruled, the exchange proceeds, has always
been the first step to intercommunity of social
and, ultimately, of civil rights.

In fact, the impossibility of long denying
class-equality to the worshippers in the same
temple, the partakers of the same rites, is not
less certain than is, unfortunately, the extreme
difficulty—I would fain hope not impossibility—
of maintaining that same equality where the
rites are diverse and the temples apart. Did I
hear any one say something that sounded like
"Ireland"?—if so, it was you that said it, my
dear sir, not I. Let us look for our illustrations
in the East; it is safer ground.

That no Mahometan can be rightfully made a
slave of, that an enslaved "unbeliever" becomes,
if he embraces Mahometanism, entitled to freedom after the lapse of seven years, are axioms of
Mahometan law, acknowledged, in theory, as
binding by every Islamitic nation, though too
often violated in practice. And indeed they
have been generally, if not exactly, observed for
many centuries; and hence throughout Turkey,
Egypt, Arabia, and the Levant we see the
liberated negro, in spite of all prejudices of
colour and race, occupying precisely the same
social position as the whites around him, with no
drawback except such as his own mental or
moral shortcomings may individually impose.

Our Surinam colonists of two hundred years
since had probably little knowledge of the
Mahometan world, and the results of Asiatic
experience; but they instinctively felt that to
admit their slaves, even nominally, to a fellow-
ship of creed would only be the first step
towards ulterior "levelling up"; that equality
in the Courts of the Temple would soon be
followed by equality in the Court of Justice, and,
finally, in the Court of Policy itself; in a word,

that the one existing ideal barrier being removed, no matter-of-fact fence could be erected strong enough to supply its wants. Certainly, no one acquainted with those whom our ancestors termed "churchmen" would suppose that the stipendiary ministers of a state religion were likely to compromise their own position by making themselves the champions of negro souls *versus* planters' interest, whatever might be the possible advantages, according to their own theory, to the negro souls aforesaid; and accordingly, for more than a century, the negroes on the banks of Surinam, Commeweyne, Cottica, Perica, and the rest, remained, for belief and worship, in the precise condition of their fathers on the African West Coast. Of this state of things a sample yet remains in the maroons, or Bush negroes, of the interior, the majority of whom are even now Nature-worshippers after the old African form. But, towards the middle of the last century, the modification of public feeling, which was in due time to render first the slave-trade, and then slave-holding itself, an impossibility and an abhorrence, had begun to make its appearance, not only in England, but among the more civilized nations of Europe generally, and through them penetrated across the seas to the slave-owning colonies of the West. And here the first link to be undone in the chain of bondage was, of course, that of religious disparity. But who should loosen it? Clearly not the ministers of any national and established Church, Dutch or English; themselves the thralls of interest and society, their own hands were too closely tied for untying the hands of others. The work was one for the irregular, not the uniform-wearing, soldiers of Christianity; and they were not long in entering on the field.

More fortunate than their compeers of Jamaica and its sister islands, the Surinam slaves fell to the share of the Moravian teachers, who had already, as far back as 1735, organized settlements among the Indians of the interior with much labour and little result. It is remarkable that almost the only teachers who have met with any success—and, indeed, their success, so to call it, has been considerable—among the Indians of the two continents, south and north, are Roman Catholic priests. A sensuous idolatry best fits a sensuous good-for-nothing race. Whereas, when a

Catholic missionary suggested to a Bush negro, the other day, the propriety of exchanging his hereditary worship of the Cotton-tree for that of an imaged Virgin Mary or some other saintly doll, the black is reported to have answered, "God made our idol; man made yours; and, besides, ours is the finer of the two"; and accordingly declined the exchange. "*Se non e vero, e ben trovato.*"

But to return to the Moravians. When, after some difficulty, though less than might have been anticipated from the nature of things, on the masters' part, they were allowed to turn their attention to the slaves, their success was as rapid as it was well deserved. In 1776 the first negro was baptized, and admitted as a member of the congregation; and the countenance publicly and generously given on the occasion by the Governor of the colony marked this step with the importance of an historical event. The very same year a Moravian teaching-establishment was opened on one of the Commeweyne estates; others followed, and, long before the emancipation of 1863, three-fourths of the working negroes had been numbered in the Moravian ranks. The

latest census gives nineteen Moravian schools,
attended by more than 2,200 children, while over
24,000 names, all Creole, are inscribed in the
register of the Herrnhut Brotherhood.

With the intrinsic merits or defects of discipline
or dogma in the Moravian system, which may be
concisely described as the exactest reproduction
known to our times of primitive Christianity,
taken in its better phases, I have nothing here to
do. These are matters of opinion, and every
man has his own. It is not the theory, but the
practical result that claims our attention; and,
allowances duly made for circumstances and the
inevitable defects and errors of every human
institution, whatever its range, this result is
eminently satisfactory, both to the people and
the colony at large.

That the emancipation, too long deferred, of
1863 was neither preceded, accompanied, nor
followed in Dutch Guiana by any disturbances
like those which agitated Jamaica, Demerara,
and other settlements thirty years before; that
apprenticeship, so signal a failure elsewhere, here
proved a success; that when this, too, came to
its appointed end in 1873, scarcely one among the

thousand of creole labourers on the estates struck work, or took advantage of his new completeness of freedom to give himself up to idleness and vagabond life,—these things are mainly due, so the colonists acknowledge, to the spirit of subordination, industry, and order inspired into their pupils by the Moravian teachers. Alike untinctured by Baptist restlessness and Methodist fanaticism, their loyalty and good sense had prepared a people worthy of the rights, into the enjoyment of which they at last entered; they had made of the slaves under their tutorial care, not only, as the phrase goes, good Christians, but they had also made of them what the majority of other teachers had failed to do, good citizens and good subjects, loyal to their government, respectful to their superiors, orderly among themselves. Obeah and poisoning, serious crimes, indeed, in any form, are almost unknown in Dutch Guiana; camp-meetings, and the disgraceful extravagances of "native Baptist" preachers, mountebanks, and demagogues, entirely so.

Liberty of conscience, and the freedom of every man to choose and follow whatever reli-

K

gion he will, are very good things; yet even their warmest supporter would hardly hesitate to bring up his children, by preference, in that form of religion to which he himself belongs. Negroes, in their present phase, are children—when newly emancipated they might have been more properly termed babies; and there would certainly have been then no harm, nor even much difficulty, in prescribing for them some one of the many modes of Christianity best adapted to their comprehension and capabilities. And, of all modes, the Moravian, with its simple creed, simple though emotional worship, strict discipline, and absence of priestly casteship, would, I venture to think, have been the best.

These reflections, which, so far as they are merely reflections, the reader-companion of my trip is free to adopt or reject as he pleases, have in this, my narrative, derived their origin from the sight of the barn-like buildings of the Moravian establishment called the Charlottenburg, alongside of which we are now borne on the clear black depths of the Cottica. The high-roofed, conventual-looking mansion occupied by the teachers themselves has a somewhat German

air; the chapel school-house and cattle-sheds—
from which last, with garden-cultivation and
farming-work on a small scale, the "mission" is
chiefly supported—are all spacious and all plain
even to ugliness. If we enter the buildings, we
shall see little more, or, in truth, nothing whatever,
to gratify the artistic sense. Within, as without,
any approach to ornamentation—not decorative
only, but architectural even—is strictly excluded,
though whether for reasons of economy or on
some abstract principle I do not know. Perhaps it is a speculative "craze;" for why should
not the Moravians have crazes of their own, like
other denominations? However, as this fancy—
if fancy it be—does not interfere with the practical utility of the constructions, which are cool,
roomy, well aired, and well kept, want of beauty
may be pardoned, though deplored. The interior arrangements, too, offer nothing to make a
description interesting. A school-room—an elementary one especially—is much the same all the
world over, whether the scholars be black or
white; and the same may be said of a meeting-
house and its contents. But, as I have already
said, they answer the purposes they were in-

tended for, and, in addition, they really come up to the popular idea. Private dwellings, by African rule of taste, should be small—mere sleeping-coverts, in fact—with an open verandah or shed tacked on, it may be, but as little construction as possible. Public buildings, on the contrary, cannot be too large. For decoration, the African eye has no great discernment; it appreciates bright colours and their combinations, but that is nearly all. In form—imitative form especially—they are at the very first letter of the Art-alphabet; nor were the most gifted of their kind, the ancient Egyptians, much further advanced in either respect. What, then, can be expected from the West Coast national type? But, like the princes of their brotherhood, the light-coloured Africans of the Nile valley, the Congo negro and the naturalized South American creole, understand the value of size in architecture as well as Mr. Ferguson himself, though not equally able perhaps to give the reason of the value; and the spacious assembly-room and wide enclosure of a Central African palace or a Surinam negro meeting-place are the legitimate, though somewhat feeble and degenerate, descendants of the giant structures of Edfou and Carnac.

Cottages and gardens extend far away to the right and left of the open space where stands the central establishment; while cocoa-nut trees form a conspicuous and a very agreeable figure in the general landscape. Sir Charles Dilke asserts, correctly, I take for granted, that 200,000 acres of Ceylon land are shaded by cocoa palms yielding from seven to eight hundred million cocoa-nuts a year, and worth two millions sterling. Amen. There is no reason, or, to put it better, no hindrance, either of climate or soil, to prevent the mainland Dutch settlement of the west from rivalling or excelling, in this respect, the once Dutch island of the east. Nor is much labour, nor much expense, beyond the first outlay of planting, required. Yet even for these men and capital are alike wanting. Well, everything has its day; and Surinam, when her time comes, may be the garden of Guiana: she is for nineteen-twentieths of her extent more like the shrubbery now.

Meanwhile the current and the boat are bearing us on round another curve of the bank; the glittering plantain screen and the infinite inter-

lacings of the cocoa-leaves have closed round the
green gap with its long-roofed buildings; last of
all, the small painted belfry has, so to speak, been
swallowed up among the boughs, and "all the
landscape is remade." Here is a remarkably
large and handsome residence, with an avenue
down to the water's edge, and landing-place to
match; the garden, too, and the statues amid
its flowers look more numerous and more fantastic
than common; the factory is in good working
order, the sheds full of megass, the out-houses
stocked; everything betokens a prosperous condition. The negroes at the wharf salute us with flags,
popguns, and what they are pleased to call singing, as we approach. I inquire the name of the
place: it is Munnikendam, the Governor informs
me; adding that the estate is remarkable for the
conservative tenacity with which, amid all the
changes that have from time to time come over
the spirit of the colonial dream, it has maintained
unchanged old customs, old feelings, old manners
and modes of life. Certainly we are now, in
what may be termed an out-of-the-way corner,
not far from the very extreme limits of European
habitation; and central influences may have been

slow in diffusing themselves by Dutch barges up
this secluded winding river. Nevertheless, to my
English eye the busiest districts of the colony and
the capital itself had already appeared remarkably conservative. Not wholly stationary, for
progress there certainly is; but it is progress by
line and rule, precept and measure—here a little,
and there a little,—not on the sweeping scale or
by the rapid transitions ordinary in the empirical
regions of the New World. So that, thought I,
if Paramaribo be comparatively not conservative,
the conservation of Munnikendam must be something worth the studying. The Governor assented;
and by his order a message was shouted across
the stream that on our return we would pay the
good folks of the estate a visit; and we continued
our way.

My readers will, I hope, accompany us on our
visit to Munnikendam in the following chapter,
and derive from it as much pleasure in idea as we
ourselves did in actual fact. Just now, however, the
immediate goal to which we were bound was the
estate entitled " La Paix," the remotest of all
European settlements or farms from the colonial
centre, bordering on what was once the military

frontier, between which and the Maroweyne river
the land lies yet open and unreclaimed. East of
the Maroweyne commences Surinam's old rival
and plunderer, French Cayenne. The distance of
" La Paix " from the capital in a straight line is
about fifty miles ; following the river windings,
it cannot be much short of a hundred.

The Cottica, in this part of its course, and above
its junction with the Perica, which flows into it a
little below Munnikendam, is narrow, often not
exceeding eighty yards in width, but extremely
deep ; the banks, where they have not been
cleared for cultivation, or planted over with fruit
trees, are a tangled maze of forest, underwood,
creeper, leaf, flower, thorn, through which a cat
or a snake could hardly find a way. Coffee-
bushes, the abandoned relics of plantation, mingle
freely with the native growth ; tall palms shoot
up everywhere; bamboo tufts bend gracefully over
the stream ; water-lilies, pink, white, and yellow,
float on the ink-black waters. From space to
space, the opening of some small natural creek or
artificial creek enlarges the vista, green and
flower-starred to its furthest reach. Amid these
Creole cottages and gardens, cocoa-nut and banana

plantations, abound and prosper; there is no sign
of insecurity anywhere, still less of want. A
mile or so before we reach "La Paix" we pass
the large dwelling-house called "Groot Marseille."
It is inhabited by three creole negroes, the joint
proprietors of the adjoining sugar estate; and
these land-owning brethren, though thriving, live
together, strange to say, in unity.

La Paix itself, with its 1,760 acres of grant,
though not more than one-third of them are under
actual cultivation, is a fine sugar estate; the
fertility of the soil is evidently only limited by
the amount of labour bestowed on it; and the
employment of coolies speaks well for the
corresponding amount of capital invested. Yet
the place has a half wild frontier look; and in the
struggle between the industry of man and the
excessive productiveness of nature, the latter
seems ever and anon almost on the point of gain-
ing the upper hand. Long grass and fantastic
undergrowth shoot up wherever the smallest
vacancy is left; the cane-patch shows like a little
island surrounded by an encroaching tide of trees;
and the tall branches, overshadowing cottage
and outhouse, give the habitations a backwood-

settlement appearance, doubtful and undecided. And here, on the twilight verge, where the extremest rays of civilization blend with the dark margin of savage or, at any rate, non-civilized existence beyond, let us pause awhile, before we step on shore, and listen to the strange story of those strange tribes on whose frontiers we now are—the Bush negroes of Surinam.

CHAPTER V.

BUSH NEGROES.

We, boys, we
Will die fighting, or live free.

BYRON.

THE groups that had gathered to greet us as we landed at the large wooden " stelling " in front of " La Paix " had an appearance not unbefitting the general character of the place itself. Mixed together, yet distinct, the slender, ornament-circled limbs and cringing gestures of the turbaned coolies by the wharf contrasted strangely with the sturdy forms and independent demeanour of the Bush negroes, here present in great force, mixed up with the more disciplined creoles, many of whom were, however, scarcely more overburdened with apparel, or, rather, sensible of the want of it, than their Maroon kinsmen around. There was no lack of that general good feeling and willing subordination that characterize the more civilized population nearer the capital. All were cheerful—the coolies, perhaps, excepted, but cheerfulness is not a Hindoo virtue either at home or abroad—and courteous after a fashion, but somewhat wild.

A painted four-oar boat, with its commodious stern cabin, the overseer's conveyance, lay alongside the wharf; two broad, flat-bottomed barges were moored some way up the main creek that leads to the interior of the estate; and, besides these, were a dozen Maroon corials, mere hollow tree-trunks, the simplest forms of barbaric invention, "survivals," to borrow Mr. Tylor's excellent nomenclature, of a pre-civilized era in river navigation.

The owners of the corials, tall, well-shaped men of colour, varying between dark brown and inky black, with a rag, at most, bound turban-fashion round their bullet heads, and another of scarce ampler dimensions about their loins, muster on the landing-place, and salute the Governor with a courteous deference to which the fullest uniform could add nothing. The women, whose dress may best be described as a scanty kilt, and the children, boys and girls, who have none to describe, keep somewhat in the back-

ground, laughing of course. All seem perfectly
at home, without strangeness or even shyness of
any kind. Nor, indeed, are they strangers from
far off; their villages on the banks of the Upper
Cottica itself, and of its tributary stream, the
Coermotibo, are almost contiguous to the European estates. The main body of the tribe is,
however, far away on the banks of the Saara
river, to the south, where their chief resides, and
along the west bank of the Maroweyne, the
boundary river between Dutch and French
Guiana. All this vast region, said, by the few
explorers who have visited it, to be in no respect
inferior for its fertility and the variety of its products to the best lands of Surinam, has been
made over, partly by express treaty, partly by
custom, to the maroons, commonly known as the
Aucan Bush negroes, the first who, in 1761,
obtained a formal recognition of freedom and
independence from their European masters. Of
the entire district they are now almost the sole
occupants, undisturbed even by dark-skinned
competitors; for the Indian aborigines, believed
to have been once numerous throughout these
wooded valleys, have wasted away and disap-

peared, unable not merely to compete but even to co-exist with their African, any better than with their European neighbours. A small Dutch settlement, that of Albina, on the banks of the Maroweyne, alone varies the uniformity of negro possession in these lands.

It was not till after a long struggle and much bloodshed that the Aucan negroes established themselves as the recognized lords of the soil. Nor would they, it is more than probable, have succeeded in doing so, but for the same causes that first determined and gave importance to their revolt—French hostilities and border-war. That a strong rival feeling should, from the very first, have existed between the Dutch and French colonies was natural enough; they were rivals, and local rivalry could not but, in their case, be embittered and intensified by the long-standing hostility between the mother-countries themselves. In the New World, however, as in the Old, it is but justice to the Dutch to say that, not they, but the French were the aggressors.

Border raids, sometimes in concert with the action of the French fleet along the coast, but in general more harassing than dangerous, kept

the Dutch settlement, from the Maroweyne on the
east, as far as the central river of Surinam, in a
condition of constant disquietude for many years;
and while they weakened the planters, encouraged
the ever-growing spirit of insubordination among
the slaves. Runaways multiplied, and, joining
together in small robber-bands, helped the French
plunderers in their work of devastation; till, not
much after the commencement of the eighteenth
century, Cassard's terrible invasion, after nearly
involving the entire colony in immediate and
irretrievable ruin, only retired to leave behind it
a long train of social and financial evils, and,
worst of all, a servile war.

That such a war must, sooner or later, have
arisen, the normal circumstances of the colony,
even had it been absolutely free from outward
pressure or accidental difficulties, suffice to show.
The number of negroes, mostly stout, able-bodied,
and with every feeling of natural hatred against
their iniquitous captors yet fresh in their breasts,
already exceeded 20,000 ; while there is no reason
to suppose that the total of European residents in the
colony ever overpassed one-tenth of that amount.
So overwhelming a majority of blacks, however

ignorant and unprovided with the artificial means
of strength wielded by their employers, could, of
course, be only retained in bondage by a persistent system of extreme severity; and severity
was sure to degenerate in many, if not most,
instances, into downright and wanton cruelty,
thus daily adding new motives of revenge to
what might have already seemed more than
sufficient. True, the Dutch were not exceptionally
hard masters; they might even, as a whole, contrast favourably with many other slave-owning
nationalities of the time. But the very tale,
briefly told a few pages back, of the lawlessness
that all the energy of Van Sommelsdyk for a time
failed to suppress, and the savage mutiny in which
he lost his life, gives evidence enough, that however temperate, orderly, and law-abiding may
have been the leaders of the brave Zeelanders
who founded Surinam, they could not but have
numbered among the ranks of their followers
many rough-handed, turbulent, lawless men,
impatient of power in the hands of others, and
sure to abuse it when holding it in their own.
Even with the better sort, it could hardly, sooner
or later, be otherwise. "Never had man absolute

power over man, but he misused it," says the
Eastern proverb ; it might, for the truth of its
application, be a Western one too. There is no
need to examine further; the history of slavery
and slaves, no less than of slave-owners, is the
same everywhere—the worst blot on the pages of
time. Alike monotonous in horror is its only
episode, insurrection.

Within a small insular inclosure, like Barbados,
or even a larger one, such as Jamaica, a negro
outbreak, however vigorous and well concerted,
was sure to yield, most often speedily, at all
events surely, to regular troops and the superiority of European skill. But in a territory of
undefined extent, backed on every side by an
untracked extent of river forest, insurgents had,
and were not long in perceiving that they had, a
very different and much better prospect of
success; and the Surinam negroes might reasonably hope that the issues of a war in which all
the disadvantages were on the side of the regular
troops, the advantages on their own, would be
for them, if not in conquest, at least in freedom.
They wanted but the occasion to begin; it came,
and it was Cassard who brought it.

L

When the French marauders of 1712-13 over-
spread the land, and chiefly the eastern Commeweyne districts, many of the planters fled for
refuge to the capital, leaving their negroes to
shift for themselves. That they did; and did it
after a fashion that common sense should have
told their owners to expect. Joining themselves
to the invaders, they helped to plunder the
abandoned estates; took what they could, and
then, quitting for ever the hated scenes of their
past miseries and wrongs, retreated to freedom
and savage life in the bordering forests. Here
they became a nucleus of avowed revolt, daily
augmented by fresh arrivals from other estates;
while, encouraged by their example, new bands of
runaways gathered and grew in all directions;
till from east, west, and south, from the Saramacca
to the Maroweyne and the uplands far away,
land-owners and colony were girt in by a ring
of desperate freebooters, eager for plunder and
ruthless with revenge. Like whirlwind gusts
bursting all at once from a murky horizon, they
broke in when least looked for upon every plantation within their range, lent their too efficient
aid to every uprising of their bondsmen-comrades,

and their cutlasses to every massacre of their
terrified and outnumbered lords.

Dr. Johnson, than whom, when unblinded by
prejudice, no better hater of injustice and wrong
ever lived, once, at a public dinner, startled, we
are told, the assembled city worthies by the un-
expected toast, "To the next negro rising in
Jamaica!" And stranger still, the toast, as it
appears, was responded to. For, in truth, it is
hard not to sympathize, from a distance especially,
with the slave against his master, the weak
against the strong, the victim against the tyrant.
Who has not read and, reading, approved
Cowper's spirited protest?—

"Patience itself is meanness in a slave.
Or if the will and sovereignty of God
Bid suffer it awhile and kiss the rod,
Wait but the dawning of a brighter day,
And snap the chain the moment when you may."

But warfare of whatever kind, however glorious
as a whole, is sickening in its details; and most
sickening of all are the details of servile war—
cruelty requited with cruelty, horror with horror.
The customary restraints imposed by common
humanity on the excited passions of the com
L 2

batants, the mitigations of civilized forbearance,
have here no place ; in the struggle the wounded
finds no pity, the captive no mercy, the dead no
honour; even the scientific interest that belongs
to the tactics and manœuvres of ordinary warfare
is wanting here; till Cicero's cowardly, " Better
peace on the worst terms than war on the best,"
almost finds an echo in the mind of the reader
who is compelled to wade through the weary
sameness of forays, ambushes, plunderings,
burnings, tortures, executions, reprisals, revenges,
that make up the hateful tale.

Enough, then, to say that the raids of the
self-emancipated marauders, after fifteen years of
ever-increasing frequency, were, in 1730, brought
to a climax by the first general rising on record
among the slaves themselves. It broke out on
the Government plantation of " Berg-en-Daal "
("Hill and Valley"), on the Upper Surinam river,
and thence extended to the neighbouring estates;
and though, after three years of hard fighting, the
insurgents yielded at last to the regular troops,
the respite obtained by the colonists was only
a temporary one. Before long the war—for it
was now no less—between whites and blacks

raged fiercer than ever, until a formal treaty, concluded by Captain Creutz in the name of the
Dutch Government, with 1,600 armed rebels,
raised the latter in 1749 to the dignity of
recognized belligerents. It is worthy of record,
not only for the justification of Governor
Mauricius, the originator of this treaty, and who
was much blamed for it at the time, but more as
affording an instance of a marked and persistent
difference between the African and the Asiatic
character, that in the present and in every
following instance the negroes observed their
part of the engagements entered into with
scrupulous fidelity. It was well for Surinam they
did so.

But the 1,600 included in the treaty were a
mere handful compared with the ever-growing
multitudes of unpacified insurgents, who, under
the leadership of their dreaded chief, Samsam,
continued the struggle with varying results, till
the impolitic severity of the owner of an estate
on the Tempatic creek, a confluent of the Upper
Commeweyne, brought about in 1757 a general
rising of the slaves throughout the southern
districts, and gave a formidable accession of

strength to the negro cause. The new insurgents, sensible of the importance of combination, joined themselves to those already in the field, and the united army put itself under the command of a competent leader. The name of this black Spartacus was Arabee—an indication that he, like his predecessor Samsam, belonged to one or other of the Mahometanized African tribes, whose national training, the result of contact with the higher races of their continent, gives them a decided superiority over their pagan fellow-countrymen, especially in war.

Had the negroes now made full use of their advantages, a general massacre of all the whites then within the colony, followed in due course by the most terrible retaliation from the enraged Dutch, might have been the result, alike disastrous to both parties—colonists and slaves. But, fortunately for Surinam, the insurgents had found in Arabee a leader whose moderation equalled his courage, and whose foresight inclined him to prefer a permanent and honourable security to the tempting but delusive gratifications of revenge. Instead of pushing forward hostilities to their utmost, he took the first offered oppor-

tunity to open negotiations of peace on equal
terms with the Colonial Government, and at last
succeeded in obtaining for himself and his followers, not only liberty and independence, but
even an extensive grant of territory to be held in
full right, on condition of an alliance offensive
and defensive with their former masters. This
treaty, of which no subsequent breach is recorded
on either side, was after some delay solemnly
concluded and sworn to at Auka, a plantation on
the shores of the Upper Surinam river, in the year
1761; and to this circumstance the associated
negroes owe the name of Aucans, which they
have ever since retained as a tribal denomi-
nation, distinguishing them from their fellows of
the bush. To these Aucans belonged our stalwart, unclad, but not uncourteous or even wholly
uncivilized friends, who, in company with their
more domesticated creole brethren, now welcomed
us on the Upper Cottica, at the landing-place of
" La Paix."

Masses, unlike individuals, are not less readily
influenced by good example than by bad; and
hardly had the Aucans made their peace with
Government when a message arrived at Paramaribo

from another considerable body of insurgents, those, namely, who occupied the uplands along the Saramacca river to the east, intimating their desire for a like peaceful settlement of affairs. The Dutch Government, with a wise leniency, at once acceded to their wish; and Louis Nepveu, an enterprising and talented official, who himself some years later became Governor of the colony in difficult times, was deputed to negotiate a treaty, similar in all respects to that concluded with the Aucans. This he accomplished in 1762; and the honours with which he was rewarded by a grateful Administration did not exceed the merit of his services. The pacification of the two great rebel clans, and the repression of the few remainining insurgents, whom the Aucans and Saramaccan negroes, mindful of their recent engagements, now joined with the European soldiery in putting down, seemed to guarantee long years of rest and prosperity to Dutch Guiana.

But the calm was delusive. The very next year a storm, more dangerous than any of the preceding ones, burst on the much-tried colony This time it was not with the negroes of the distant up-country districts, not with the labourers on the scattered and unimportant plantations, but with the slaves who tilled the close-packed, wealthy coast estates, the very mainstay and life of the settlement, that the Dutch had to contend. Along the entire sea-shore, from the mouth of the Saramacca on the west, where the strong post of Nassau Fort was abandoned and blown up by its fugitive garrison, to the mouth of the Maroweyne east, one only estate, the Government plantation, called Dageraad, resisted the insurgents, and by its central position prevented a junction of their forces that might well have been fatal to Paramaribo itself. Had Dageraad fallen, the colony, cut off from the seabord and deprived of all hope of succour from without, must have perished. Now it was that the treaties so lately concluded with the Aucan and Saramacca negroes stood the colony in good stead; the inland region behind the capital remained undisturbed and faithful; and thus the garrison of Paramaribo found itself sufficiently at leisure to detach a small body of European troops to the help of their besieged comrades in Dageraad. They arrived only just in time; but Dageraad was saved, and with it the

colony. Succour, first from St. Eustatius, then
in greater numbers from Holland, now came in;
the insurgents lost heart; and by the summer of
the following year the worst of the peril was
over. But it was not followed by peace. This,
for once, was neither sought nor granted; and
the blood poured forth in the numerous executions which signalled the first repression of the
revolt, though for a moment they damped, could
not quench the flame. Now smouldering, now
bursting into open blaze, it continued to ravage
the easterly districts along the valleys of the
Commeweyne and its tributary rivers, where
property and life were held on no securer tenure
than they had been, twenty years previously, on
the Upper Surinam and the frontiers of the south.
But the character of the revolt had changed from
purely servile to semi-political; for foreign influences were really, though indirectly, at work,
circumscribing, while they embittered, the contest. The chiefs of the new freebooters, Bonni
and Baron, had established their head-quarters
near the Maroweyne river, on the French frontier,
within which the connivance of the Cayenne
Government seemed to afford them, whenever

hard pressed, a secure place of refuge, and whence they also drew fresh recruits and supplies at need.

Eight years passed thus, during which time many expeditions were undertaken by the European troops against the insurgents; but, owing to the difficulties of the marshy coast-grounds and the neighbourhood of the French territory, with little effect. In 1770, Louis Nepveu assumed the government, and, with the aid of a distinguished officer, Colonel Stoelman by name, organized a black corps, recruited from among the negroes themselves—a measure productive of the greatest advantages, and which sufficiently indicates the change that had come over the spirit of the contest, and the altered relations of the combatant parties. It was no longer a struggle between black and white, but between rebel and Dutch. Negroes though they were, Bonni and Baron were regarded as enemies by the Africans, no less than by the European subjects of the State; and the blacks at large proved themselves, then and ever after, loyal to the Netherlands flag, nor less ready to fight under it than the Zeelanders themselves.

Now was the time for putting the revolt, thus
localized and extra-national, completely down;
and at last, in 1773, the earnest and long-conti-
nued representations made by Governor Nepveu
to the States succeeded in obtaining a reinforce-
ment of 800 Dutch soldiers, commanded by
Colonel Fourgeoud, a Swiss by birth, and a man
of considerable military merit, though quarrel-
some and overbearing in temper. With him, and
under the same flag, arrived Captain Stedman,
an Englishman and a scholar, the destined historian—and by no means an inelegant one—of
the campaign. With the arrival of Fourgeoud
and his troops, military operations commenced,
and were continued in a much more regular
manner than formerly, and with better result.
Guided and seconded by their black allies, the
European soldiers made their way into the
furthest forest recesses. Every communication
was secured, every advance rendered permanent,
by the erection of a fort; while fresh reinforce-
ments gradually raised the numbers of the negro
soldiery to about eight hundred, and those of the
Dutch troops to double the amount. An expe-
dition on so large a scale, and conducted by men

who understood their work, could not fail of success. Outgeneralled and beaten in a succession of skirmishes, Bonni, who was at this time sole rebel chief, gave up the game for lost, and, with the more obstinate spirits of his band, crossed the Maroweyne, to find permanent shelter in the territory of Cayenne. But the greater number of the insurgents, deprived of their leader, preferred to seek, and by timely submission to obtain, the same conditions of peace that had, on former occasions, been granted to the Aucan and Saramaccan tribes, with which, under the name of Bonni negroes, they became speedily incorporated; others joined the Moesinga or Matrocane clan. By the spring of 1786 the pacification was complete on all sides. And thus, after fifty years of hard fighting, ended the servile wars of Dutch Guiana.

They were never renewed. A strong military cordon of numerous and well-appointed posts, drawn round the cultivated lands, and including all the European settlements and estates, sufficed to keep at distance any chance marauding runaways, whether negroes or others, while the black soldiers, who were called " Guides " from the nature of the services originally required of them, satisfactorily supplied, for many years, the place of regular troops, and spared the exhausted colony, which had already incurred a debt amounting to 60,000,000 of florins for war cost alone, the heavy expenses of a European garrison. Beyond this cordon lay the territory definitely assigned to the Bush negroes, and from them neither danger nor disquiet had henceforth to be apprehended. Liberty alone was what they had fought for, and, having once secured that for themselves and their children, they regarded all bygone scores of slavery, ill-usage, and war as cancelled in full. Indeed the oft-cited double precept, "Forgive and forget," the first half of which is difficult enough to our European natures, and the latter impossible, is a matter of every-day practice among negroes, with whom benefit obliterates injury, or *vice versâ*, more rapidly and more completely than a Caucasian can even understand. A phenomenon indicative of a good heart, say some; of a weak head, say others. Of both perhaps. But to return to our Bush negroes.

So thoroughly did they henceforth consider their own interests identified with those of the colony at large, that when, towards the close of the century, Dutch Guiana was being bandied about, now by treaty, now by force of arms, while to-day an English, to-morrow a French flag floated over its forts, and the victors of one hour were the vanquished of the next, the Aucans and their kin, ignorant of European politics, and averse to change, whatever its pretext, came boldly forward of their own accord to the assistance of their old masters against the foreign intruders, and contributed as best they could to the defence of Surinam in difficult times.

Since then more than seventy years have gone by; and with them many of the institutions of the colony have also passed from fact to history, from history to oblivion. The military cordon, so important in its day, exists no longer; and no territorial demarcation now assigns special limits to European denizenship in Surinam. From English rule the colony has returned to Dutch, has prospered, has dwindled, and prospered again; slavery has given place to apprenticeship, and apprenticeship to the equality of freedom. Coolie immigration, produce-experiments, machinery, commerce, have each in turn modified some things, created others,

obliterated not a few. But through all these
changes the Bush negroes have remained, with
hardly any alteration, on their original footing,
true to their first engagements, at peace among
themselves, and by no means useless members of
the settlement into which they are incorporated,
half as subjects, half allies. Their mode of life is
agricultural; their labour is partly bestowed on
the field-produce sufficient to their own personal
wants, partly on the growth and export of rice,
with which they supply the estates and the capital.
But their chief occupation is woodcutting; and
their skill in this department has secured them an
almost absolute monopoly of the timber supply
that forms a considerable item in the trade-list of
Surinam. They hew, trim, divide the planks,
and do whatever is requisite for preparing the
wood for shipment; then bring it down in the
form of rafts, or boat-loads, to Paramaribo, where
they exchange it most commonly for arms, powder,
cooking utensils, and other household necessaries.
Fortunately for themselves, strong drink is not
a favourite article of barter among these unregistered and unbaptized disciples of Father
Mathew and Sir Wilfrid Lawson. Indeed, in

this, as in many other respects, they present an
advantageous contrast with the besotted Indians,
whose diminution and almost disappearance from
the land have been occasioned by intemperance,
much more than by any of the numerous causes
assigned on philo-indigenous platforms. With
the negro, on the contrary, drunkenness is an
exotic vice, and even where it has been implanted
it does not flourish largely on his soil.

Their settlements far up among the rivers,
and in regions said to be admirably adapted for
cultivation, though as yet rarely favoured by
European visitors, are grouped together after the
fashion of small villages, resembling, I am told,
in their principal features, the more accessible
hamlet inhabited by emancipated Congo Africans,
and called "Bel Air," near Berbice. Their
dwellings are reported to be neat and comfortable
enough after a fashion. About fifty of these
villages are recorded by name; the average
number of souls in each equals 300, or thereabouts. The census of the entire Bush negro
population is almost conjectural; some bring
their numbers down to 8,000, others raise them
to 30,000. Of the two extremes, the latter is, I

M

believe, the nearer to the truth. Negroes, like other Eastern tribes, when required to give an account of themselves, are in the habit of reckoning up their men only, omitting the women altogether, and even the male children, if still at the breast. Fear of taxation is another common motive for under-statement, especially in the presence of official inquiry. Every village has its chief; his office is partly hereditary, partly elective, and he himself is distinguished from his subjects by a uniform, to be worn, however, only on rare and special occasions—a fortunate circumstance in so warm a climate. He also bears a staff of office. These lesser chiefs are again under the orders of the headsman of the tribe, who has a right to wear, when he chooses,—a rare occurrence, let us hope,—a general's uniform, and to bear in his hand a bâton of rule, surmounted by a gilded knob.

The principal divisions of Bush negro nationality are three in number—Aucan, Saramaccan, and Moesinga or Matrocane, names not of ancestral, but of local origin—a circumstance alluded to before. Each group has, however, its own subdivisions, known among the tribesmen themselves, though hardly recognized by others. Thus, under the general title of Aucans are comprehended the Bonni, Paramaccan, and Poregoedoc negroes; the Luango belong to the Saramaccans; the Koffys, to the Moesingas. The three great tribes were, in fact, at their first beginnings, composed of men held together by no special link, except that of arms, taken up in a common cause. But the grouping, once made, perpetuated itself, and in the course of years it has produced in each instance a distinct type, till what was at first merely nominal and accidental has become permanent and real. Of the three clans, the Aucans rank the highest in general estimation, as being the most manly, intelligent, and industrious. That they have persistently declined to exchange their hereditary paganism for Christianity may pass for an exception to, or a confirmation of, their good qualities, according as the moralist is a disciple of the Rev. Mr. Badger or of the South Sea "Earl." Next in rank come the Saramaccans, amongst whom the Moravians have made not a few disciples; they are said to be of subtler disposition than the Aucans, but inferior to them in energy

and work. The Moesinga or Matrocane negroes
occupy the lowest place. Taken, however, all in
all, and allowing for the average amount of every-
day defects, from which human nature, civilized
or uncivilized, negro or non-negro, is rarely free,
the Bush negroes hold a good position among
men ; better, certainly, by far, than that occupied
by most of the aboriginal races of the South
American continent, or, under Fenimore Cooper's
leave, of the Northern either.

The three tribes just enumerated are to a certain degree reunited in the person of the Aucan
chief, or " Gramman," Anglicè " Grand Man," to
whom his Saramaccan and Moesinga colleagues
allow a respectful precedence, and who is, in fact,
acknowledged for the supreme head of all
Surinam Bush negroes whatsoever, though in
rank and in title rather than in power. The name
of the present dignitary is Blymaffo ; his pedigree
remounts up to Pamo, the first Aucan chief, to
whom it is duly traced through a line, not of
ancestors, but of ancestresses ; for negroes, like
Shakspeare, consider the recognition of a mother
as an easier matter than that of a father, and
their pedigrees are accordingly reckoned, not on

the paternal, but the maternal line. The "Grand Man," when appointed, is formally recognized and confirmed by the Colonial Governor, to whom he is bound to present himself in person at the capital; but his authority is on ordinary occasions of a very limited kind; and his position, though it commands respect, can rarely enforce obedience. As much may be said of the other chiefs, each of his tribe, Saramaccan or Moesinga. Frans Bonham is at this moment the fortunate holder of the former title; Noah Kroon, who also rejoices in the more African name "Edraai," reigns by the latter. However, the real and absolute ruler among the Bush negroes is neither "Edraai" nor Bonham, nor even the great Blymaffo himself, but custom—a ruler powerful even among civilized races, absolute among the uncivilized.

Besides the "Grand Man" of their own "skin," in negro phrase, each tribe enjoys or endures the presence of a European official, whom the Colonial Government appoints under the title of "Post-houder," to reside among them, and whose duties chiefly consist in settling the frequent petty contentions that arise between the villagers themselves or their neighbours, regarding rights of property or land. Most other cases, civil or criminal, fall under the jurisdiction of the tribe itself, and are decided by the unwritten code of usage, often sufficiently barbarous in the punishments that it awards; though the cruellest of all, that of burning alive, is said not to have been inflicted on any one for a generation past. It was the penalty especially reserved for sorcerers, and its discontinuance is attributed to the fact that the sorcerers have themselves, like the witches of Germany or Scotland, disappeared in our day. The truth is that the negroes themselves are less superstitious than of old, and, having discarded the imaginary crime from their belief, have also discarded the real one by which it was supplemented from their practice, just as the erasure of heresy from the catalogue of sins was immediately followed by the extinction of heretic-burning fagots. The beneficent triumphs of Rationalism, so ably chronicled by Lecky, are not confined to Europe and the European races; and the process of the suns brings wider thoughts to other men than the dwellers of the moorland by Locksley Hall.

Sorcerers, indeed, have, it is said,—though

from what cause I cannot readily determine,—
been of all times rare articles among the negro
colonists of Surinam. So too, though the large
majority of the Bush negroes are yet pagans, as
were their ancestors before them, when, cutlass
in hand, they hewed out their way to freedom,
Obeah, so notoriously wide-spread throughout
Africa, and, if report say true, not unknown in
some West Indian regions, is scarcely ever heard
of among them. Yet, did it exist in any notable
degree, it could hardly have failed, by the natural
contagion of evil, to have established itself also
among the creole blacks, their immediate neighbours and kinsmen, who are, however, in general,
remarkably free from any imputation of the
kind. Nor, again, are the Bush negroes, nowadays at least, addicted to the indiscriminate
fetish-worship so often described by modern tra-
vellers as prevalent in Africa. Perhaps they may
have been so formerly. At present the " ceiba,"
or " cotton tree," that noblest forest growth of the
West Indies, enjoys almost alone, if report says true,
the honours of negro worship, avowedly among
the Maroons, furtively in the creole villages. I
myself have often seen the traces of offerings—

fowls, yams, libations of drink, and the like—
scattered round its stem. The spirit-dweller of
its branches, thus propitiated, is said to be of an
amiable disposition, unlike his demon-brother of
the poison-tree, or Hiari, also venerated by some,
but out of fear. Idols, in the strict sense of the
term, they certainly have none ; and their rejec-
tion of Roman Catholicism, a circumstance to
which I have alluded before, is asserted to have
had, at least, for its ostensible motive their dislike of the image-worship embodied in that
system.

I would willingly indulge the charitable hope
that the Moravian Bush negro converts may possibly have acquired some kind of idea of the
virtue commonly designated, though in a restricted
use of the word, by the name of morality. It is
a virtue with which their pagan brethren are, in
a general way, lamentably unacquainted. On
principle, if the phrase may be allowed, they are
polygamists ; but the frequency of divorce
renders, it is said, the dignity of a Bush negro's
wife more often successional than simultaneous.

Indeed, their avowed laxity in this and analogous
directions is sometimes asserted, but how truly I

cannot say, to be one of the chief hindrances to
the increase of their numbers. Without going
into the particulars of an obscure and unpleasant
subject, thus much is clear, that a child which
has for its parents "no father and not much of a
mother," a normal condition of things in the Bush
negro villages, must necessarily commence the
infantile struggle for life under somewhat disad-
vantageous conditions. To this may be added a
total absence of medical practitioners—a circumstance which however might, by a cynical mind,
be rather reckoned among the counterbalancing
advantages of forest existence.

In form and stature the Bush negroes of
Surinam may rank among the best specimens of
the Ethiopian type. The men are often six feet
and more in height, with well-developed limbs
and pleasing open countenance; and the women
in every physical respect are, to say the least,
worthy of their mates. Ill-modelled trunks and
disproportioned limbs are, in fact, as rare among
them as they are common among some lighter-
complexioned races. Their colour is, in general,
very dark, and gives no token of the gradual
tendency to assume a fairer tint, that may be

observed among the descendants of negroes resident in more northerly latitudes. Their hair, too,
is as curly as that of any Niam-niam, or Darfooree
chief, or native of Senegal. I have heard it
asserted more often than once, that, by long
domicilement in the South American continent,
the negro type has a tendency to mould itself
into one approaching that of the Indian aboriginal. And something of the kind might be
looked for, if anywhere, among the Bush negroes
of the Surinam interior. But in the specimens
that I saw, and they were many, I could not
detect any such modification.

Their language is a curious and uncouth mixture. When it is analyzed, English appears to
form its basis; next on the list of contributors
comes Portuguese; then Dutch, besides a sprinkling of genuine African words thrown in at
random, and the thick, soft African pronunciation
over all. But of this jargon the negroes themselves make no use in writing, for which they
employ Dutch, thereby showing themselves, in
this respect, possessed of a truer feeling of the
fitness of things than, I regret to say, their
Moravian friends, who have taken superfluous

pains to translate books of instruction and devo-
tion into the so-called "negro language," for the
supposed benefit of their half-tamed scholars : an
instance—one amongst many—of being too practical by half. What is most practical is not
always what is most adapted to human nature,
nor what answers its purpose best;—a truth I
respectfully commend to the consideration of the
doctors of the utilitarian school.

Fortunately for the Bush negroes themselves,
their ultimate tendency in language, as in everything else, is to uniformity with the general creole
colonial type—one not of the very highest, it may
be, but much superior to the half or three-
quarters savagery in which they at present live.
Their little and, so to speak, accidental nationality is composed of elements too feeble and too
loosely put together not to be ultimately re-absorbed
into the more vigorous and better constructed
mass to which, though under differing conditions,
it once belonged. A strong centrifugal impulse
dispersed them, a century ago, on the outer ring
of the colonial orb ; the gentler but abiding
centripetal force of civilized organization is now
drawing them back to the inner circle. Old mis-

trusts and antipathies are fast wearing themselves
out in the daily contact with European life; and
contact with Europeans never fails to produce,
where negroes are concerned, first imitation, then
assimilation. So long as slavery lasted, this was,
of course, an impossibility for the Bush negroes;
it is now a mere question of time, longer or
shorter, according to the discretion and tact of
the Colonial Government itself, and we may
reasonably hope that the sagacity and moderation
by which that same Government has thus far
always distinguished itself will not fail it in this
matter either.

Freedom from taxation and internal autonomy
are the special privileges which the Bush negroes
in their present condition enjoy: by the latter
they set some store ; by the former much. On the
other hand, they are fully aware of the greater
advantages and enjoyments of a more settled and
civilized form of life than their own, and would
sacrifice much to make it theirs. The result of
the exchange would be, undoubtedly, a very
beneficial one, not only to the Bush negroes themselves, but to the colony at large. Labour is the
one great requisite of Surinam : rich in every gift

of unassisted nature, she is poor of that which
alone could enable her to make profit of these
gifts.   In these Maroon subjects of hers close at
hand, she possesses a copious and, as yet, an unemployed reserve force of labour, superior in most
respects to the coolie or Chinese article, and,
which is a main point, cheaper by far. The complete incorporation into colonial life and work of
the negro element, now comparatively isolated
and wasted in the bush, would add about a third
to the progressiveness and energy of Dutch
Surinam.

CHAPTER VI.

MUNNICKENDAM.

Not a word, a word : we stand upon our manners.
Come, strike up. (*Music : here a dance.*)

SHAKESPEARE.

WHEN Byron expanded Cowper's well-known
" England, with all her faults," and the rest, into
the graceful stanzas of that most graceful of all
his poems, 'Beppo,' winding up with his comprehensive " I like all and everything," he gave expression to the genuine conservatism that, whatever the formula and mode of utterance, constitutes
the under-depth and assigns the key-note of every
great mind. This conservatism is summed up in
two words—the one " submission," the other
" content "; the former has more in it of human
philosophy, the latter of divine.

But in some places, and amid some conditions
of life, it is almost impossible to feel contentment,
because the restlessness that characterizes them is
based, like the phases of being themselves, on

dissatisfaction, and can communicate no other
feeling by contact to the mind. A walk in the
streets of Chicago or Galata, a day of a New York
"gold market" or of a Parisian Commune, the
interior of a Stock Exchange, a Home Rule meeting, a Kenealy, a Cleon, these and their kin, all
of them things without contentment in themselves,
the results of disquiet, the embodiments of un-
rest, have only power to disturb and vex while
they are present, and long after, in their remem-
brance, mar, like inharmonious notes, the concert
of the past. Nor, again, is the feeling of contentment compatible with mere stagnation and listless
quiet. Little enough is to be met with of restlessness in the streets of a central Anatolian city,
says Sivas, or in the sailorless port of Sidon, or
among the sand-strewn ruins of Egyptian Thebes;
but of such like scenes the mental result is commonly depression, deepening at times into melancholy gloom. Too little life is almost—I will not
say quite—as bad as too much: screaming discord is intolerable; but dead silence is not either
what we want. It is where life abounds, but life
regulated by moderation and law,—where movement is continuous, not spasmodic and unequal,—

where progress has way, but along the steady
lines of order, not down the ringing, jarring
grooves of change,—where the present is enough
for the day, and the morrow is promised " as
to-day, and much more abundant," for the very
reason that it is the continuation of to-day,—that
contentment exists, and can be found by those
who seek it, and when found enjoyed.

So " huzza," not " for Otaheite," but for Munnickendam, of which I have already said that it
had been pronounced by the competent authority
of his Excellency the Colonial Governor the
most conservative "institution" in conservative
Surinam. Nor need my Liberal readers, if I am
honoured by such, start aside, in horror of a name,
from the easy companionship of my tale. By
" conservative" I mean—I mean—well, I do not
mean anything connected with either side of the
House : my use of the word is purely philosophi-
cal, not political ; and if it were political, why
they who, with Pope, " know like Whig minister
to Tory," may forgive : where no allusion is intended, no offence should be taken.

Bush negroes are fine fellows of their kind, I
have seldom seen finer; Indians are, within cer-

tain limits, picturesque; Chinese, if not orna-
mental, are decidedly useful; and coolies, though
not unfrequently neither, are sometimes both.
But, after all said, to be innocuous is the Indian's
highest praise; and any notable increase in West
Indian lands of "Celestials" is—for reasons not
all celestial, but much the reverse—not a thing
to be desired; while coolies are expensive to
import, and as settlers offer but a dubious future
at best. Negroes, with all their defects, are now,
as of old times, West Indian labour's best hope;
and since "salt-water" blacks and purchased
gangs are no longer to be had, creole negroes
must to the fore. In this view, if in no other,
they are worth study, and where can we study
them better than at Munnickendam?

Digression is a fault; I know it; but it is a pet
fault of mine, and, like other things under the
sun, has its time: let me indulge it here a little
longer. Besides, what I am writing is not a
guide-book, nor a narrative, nor an essay, in
any one of which I grant that digression would
be unpardonable; it is, if you will allow the
word, and be content to take it in a purely meta-
phorical sense, a sketch-book; and the arrange-

N

ment of sketches is a mere matter of convenience,
not of principle. And here I would like, though
I am not going to do it, to insert a sketch of the
little village—not so little neither—near Bel Air,
on the way to Berbice, where live the liberated
Congoites, or Congoese, or Congonians, rescued
by our cruisers from the slave-ships to which they
had already been consigned, and brought hither
at a recent date. It is a village absolutely
picturesque in its details, and, what is perhaps
more to the purpose, it offers to view, in itself and
in its garden surroundings, abundant evidence of
industry, skill, and the manly independence that
lives by its own labour, and is content to live so.
Another sketch, too, I would willingly give, that
of the new quarter of Paramaribo—the one, I
mean, situated on the westernmost outskirts of
the town, and called "the Plain of the 13th
May." That date last year was the jubilee of
the Dutch King's reign, and to celebrate the
occasion the Governor had offered prizes to the
negro workmen who would best excel in laying
out the roads and digging the trenches of the
proposed suburb. It was opened on the day itself,
with great pomp and ceremony, and distribution

of rewards, by his Excellency in person, and
was at once made over to its present inhabitants,
a class resembling in every respect the tenants of
Bel Air. A pretty patchwork of cottages and
gardens, well-doing diligent freemen to maintain
them in order and comfort—a sight to justify the
pride that its originator takes in it—a successful
experiment, on a small scale indeed, but arousing
a wish for more.

And this is exactly what not I only, but every
landowner, every proprietor, every planter in the
colony would wish to see, namely, a greater
abundance of villages and settlements like those
just described, only to a wider purpose, and on a
larger scale. Certainly I have no desire to dis-
parage the good qualities of the slave-descended
black creoles, or to join in the vague outcries,
contradicted everywhere by facts, that ignorance,
and still more prejudice, have raised against them.
But this much must be allowed, that, from the
very circumstance of being slave-descended, they
bear, and long will bear, traces of the deteriora-
ting process to which they have been subjected in
the persons of their ancestors—a deterioration
not moral merely, but mental and even physical.

In fact, their rapid, though as yet only partial, recovery from this very degradation is one proof, among many, of the wonderful elasticity of the negro character. Hesiod, if I remember rightly, or, if not he, some other old coeval Greek, has said, "When Jupiter makes a man a slave, he takes away half his brains from him"; and a truer thing was never said or sung. Cowardice, duplicity, dislike of labour, a habit of theft, sexual immorality, irreflectiveness, apathy, these are the seven daughters of slavery; and they but too often live persistently on, though their ill mother be dead for generations past. Hence the negro who has never been a slave, or who at any rate has never experienced that most crushing form of slavery, the organized task-mastership of a foreign and superior race, has a decided vantage-ground, not over his enslaved fellow-countrymen, but over the descendants of such, on whom his father's sins, and still more the sins of his father's masters, are, by hereditary law, visited even to the third and the fourth generation.

Now, assuming that of all races the negro is by physical constitution the best adapted to the

South American tropics, and that negro labour
is, of all others, not the cheapest merely, but also
the most efficient in this soil, both of which
are propositions that few experienced planters
or overseers will dispute, why not organize
emigration from Africa to the West Indies after
a regular and durable fashion? and as the East
African races are undoubtedly superior alike in
mind and body to the Western, why not establish
an emigration-agency on the east coast?—why not,
to fix a locality, at Zanzibar? Have we not lately
closed in principle, and shall soon, by means of
our cruisers, have closed in fact and deed, the
East African slave-trade, doing thereby a deed
worthy of England, worthy of ourselves? True;
and we look at our work, and justly pronounce it
to be "very good." But what if some of the
immediate results of our work, in order to be
rightly called "very good," also require careful
management, and the dexterity that not only
destroys what is bad, but replaces it by something
better? Have we not, while forbidding the
further outpourings of the poison-stream that
has for ages flowed in tears and blood from the
ports of the East African coast, driven back, in

a manner, the bitter waters to eddy on themselves, and, while stopping a recognized outlet
of the unemployed and superabundant population—a wasteful and a wrongful one it is true,
yet an outlet—created a novel surplus in the
inland African labour-market, where violence and
captivity are the only laws of exchange and
supply? Have we not also, while depriving
Zanzibar of its hateful but long-established
trade—the trade that alone gave it importance
and wealth—curtailed the revenues, and with the
revenues the very kingship, of one whose patrons
we had before consented to be, and whom we had
ourselves taught to shelter his authority, nay his
very existence, under our flag? We may have
been right—we have been right—in doing all
this; but we are not the less liable for the consequences, nor less in duty bound to obviate the
injury we may have indirectly caused, than is
the surgeon to tie up the wounds that his needful
knife has inflicted on the patient whose cure he
has taken in hand. To do evil that good may
come, is not well; but to do good so that evil,
however indirect, comes of it, is not commend-
able either.

Now, so it is that for both the evils I have
indicated—and neither of them is imaginary—a
remedy is within easy reach; a remedy not only
efficacious with regard to its immediate object,
but beneficial in its ulterior results. "Easy
reach," did I say? Yes, easy enough, if only
well-meaning ignorance will stand aside, and
have the grace to permit what it cannot comprehend. But this is a piece of good fortune to be
wished for rather than hoped; and already I
seem to hear a horrified outcry of "negro-kidnap-
ping," "disguised slavery," "slave-trade re-established," and the rest, rising from every platform, and re-echoed from every bench of the
Anti-Slavery Association and its kindred sup-
porters. What? supply the deficit of West
Indian labour by negro importation from the
east coast? Give the Seyyid, Sultan, or Sultanlet
of Zanzibar, perhaps him of Muscat too, a
nominal patronage and a real percentage of an
emigration-agency? Load ships with African
semi-slaves?—bear them, "far from home and
all its pleasures," to the coasts of Surinam, of
Demerara, of St. Vincent, &c.? What is all
this but to revive the monster we have ourselves

so lately slain; to stultify our own wisdom, annul our own decree?

Nothing of the kind, my respected friend: say, rather, it is to hinder the brood that the monster has left from coming into life, to confirm the decree of self-maintaining freedom, to complete what else, if left imperfect, might speedily bring in question the wisdom of our former deeds. It is to transfer, not by compulsion, but by their own free consent, those who, if they remain at home, cannot, by the nature of things, be other than slaves or slave-makers, to the conditions of honourable labour, self-support, and security; to bring them into the full possession of whatever benefits organized society and equitable law can confer; to substitute, so far as their own former masters are concerned, a fair and beneficial for an unjust and cruel gain; to bestow on the lands of their destination advantages that no other means, no other colonists, can equally secure.

It is certain that, if conducted under regulations and safeguards similar to those provided for the coolie emigrants of Bengal and Madras, and with the same or analogous provisions in matters of engagement, voyage, and occupation,

the unnecessary and burdensome obligation of a
return passage being alone omitted, East African
emigration would be much less costly, and at the
same time much more profitable to the colonies,
than Indian or Chinese. The negro is of himself
a better agricultural labourer than the Hindoo;
he is stronger, healthier, more readily domiciled,
more easily ruled, and, an important point, more
likely to devote himself to field and country
work after the expiration of his indentures. He
is also much less disposed than either coolie or
Chinaman to swell the town population and the
criminal list. I have said that, in his case, the
option of a return passage might be safely
omitted; for no negro, the solitary hero of Mrs.
Hemans's ballad excepted, has any great longing
to revisit his own natal land: his country is not
where he was born, but where he is well off; no
local worship, no sacred rivers, no ties of caste,
draw him back to his first home. In him, therefore, is the best, if not the only, hope of sup-
plementing the great, the urgent want of the
New World—an indigenous population; for the
Guiana Indian must, unfortunately, reckon for
nothing, either in number or in available worth; and

thus the benefit derived from him as an indentured labourer would be followed by the still more lasting benefit of an acclimatized and a useful colonist. And, to return to our friends of the Anti-Slavery Association, the evidence collected on all hands, from Anthony Trollope, after his kind, up to the Demerara Inquiry Committee in 1868, after theirs, may surely have convinced the members of that respectable body, that coolie emigration and coolie labour in the West Indies are further removed from hardship, injustice, and slavery than are too often the means by which our own agricultural labour-market is supplied, or the conditions by which it is governed. Let them, then, rest assured that the same system would have no worse result for the East African negro also.

Enough of this. The subject is one that cannot fail to be taken up sooner or later, not in speculative view, but in experimental practice; till then let it rest. Perhaps the time is not come yet; the very extent of the prospect suggests its distance. But a little sooner, a little later, not the less surely it will be reached. An African colony, the Arab, has already half peopled the East; an African law, matured in Egypt, pro-

mulgated on the shores of the Red Sea, remodelled
and repromulgated in the deserts of the same
coast, rules over half Asia this day. Already the
Libyan Sibyl prepares to turn the next page of
her book ; its writing is the West. A new creation
wanted here; and creation of this sort is a work
not for the European, or his half-cousin, the
Hindoo,—it belongs to the elder races. The
Aryan of our day, the Indo-German, can elaborate,
can perfect, he cannot originate; art-trained, art-
exhausted, the productive energy of nature is his
no longer. Unmodified by science, unpruned by
art, the rough offshoots of the ever-teeming
African stem are vital with the rude vitality of
nature ; like her, they are prolific too.

Is it a dream ? Possibly so—a nature-sent
dream, as under the hot sun we float in breeze-
less calm down the glassy black waters, between
high walls of reed and forest, bright flowers,
broad leaf, and overtopping palm, up to the intense
heaven all aglow ; till here before us, on the
left river-bank, rise the bower-like avenues
of Munnickendam. Here let us land, and from
the study of the long-settled creole negroes of
this secluded estate let us draw, if so disposed,

some augury as to what their brethren of the East African coast, the colonists of our visionary or visioned future, are likely to be in and for South-American Surinam.

This, at any rate, is no dream: 217 acres; 260 labourers, all, without exception, negro-creole; average yearly produce, 750 hogsheads of sugar, besides molasses and rum! so much for Munnickendam statistics. Machinery of the older and simple sort; factory buildings corresponding; planter's dwelling-house large, old, and three-storied, Dutch in style, with high roof, and fantastic wolves topping the gables by way of weathercocks; a wide, double flight of steps in front, with a paved space, surrounded by an open parapet, before the hall-door: the garden very Dutch in its walks, flower-beds, and statues; long avenues, some of palmiste, some of areka palm, some of almond-trees, with sago palms inter-mixed, around a green, turfy soil, and a crescent background of cane-fields and forest. So much, and enough, I think, for general description. Negroes very sturdy, very black, very plainly dressed, or half dressed in white and blue; the women rejoicing in variegated turbans; children

à la Cupid and Psyche as to costume, though not
perhaps in feature or shape; three or four white
men, overseers, straw-hatted of course; lastly, for
visitors, the Governor and his party (myself
included);—such are the principal accessories of
the picture. Time, from five or so in the afternoon to midnight, or thereabouts: we did not
very accurately consult our watches.

Night had fallen; but no,—this is a phrase well
enough adapted, it may be, to the night of the
North—the heavy, murky veil slowly let down,
fold after fold, over the pale light that has done
duty for day. Here it is not so. Transparent
in its starry clearness, its stainless atmosphere,
night rises as day had risen before,—a goddess
succeeding a goddess; not to blot out the fair
world, but to enchase it in a black-diamond circle
in place of a white—to change enchantment for
enchantment, the magic of shadow for the magic
of light. But I am anticipating. A good hour
before sunset the covered barge of the estate had
set us ashore on the wharf, where, with flowers
in their hands, songs on their lips, smiles on every
face, and welcome in every gesture, the boys and
girls of the place received us from the " stelling."

Between this double human range, that, like an
inner and more variegated avenue, lined the overarching trees from the water's edge up to the
dwelling-house, we passed along, while the merry
tumult of the assembled crowd and the repeated
discharge of the small cannon planted at the
landing-place and in the garden mingled together
to announce and greet our arrival. The warm
though almost level sunbeams lit up the red-brick
lines of the central mansion, the tall, tower-like
factory chimneys, the statues in the garden, the
pretty bush-embosomed cottages of the estate,
and tipped with yellow gold the plumy cane-fields
beyond. This lasted some time, till the sun set,
and for a little while all was orderly and still in
the quiet evening light.

But soon night had risen, and with her had
risen the white moon, near her full; and now the
merry-makers, who had dispersed to their evening
meal, re-assembled on the gravel walks and clean-
kept open spaces of the garden in front of the
dwelling-house, to enjoy the sport of the hour.
For in the West Indies as in Africa, in Surinam
no less than at Damascus, the night is the negroes'
own time; and no member of Parliament in the

later months of the session, no fashionable beauty
in her fourth London season, can more persistently invert the solar allotment of the hours
than does the negro votary of pleasure; and
wherever and however pleasure be attainable,
the negro is its votary.

Group by group, distinctly seen in the pale
moonlight as if by day, only with an indistincter
background, our creole friends flocked on. The
preparations for the dance were soon made.
Drums, fifes, a shrill violin, and a musical instrument, some say of Indian, some of negro
invention, consisting of a notched gourd, that
when scraped by a small stick gives out a sound
not unlike the chirping of a monster cricket, and
accentuates time and measure after the fashion of
triangles, were brought from heaven knows what
repositories; and with them the tuneful orchestra
was complete. The dancers ranged themselves,
more than a hundred men and women, mostly
young, all dressed in their choicest, for the night's
sport. The men, with few exceptions, were
attired in white trousers, and shirts of various
colours, with a predominance of red; some dandies
had wrapped gay sashes round their waists, and

most had provided themselves with sprigs of
flowers, jauntily stuck in their hatbands. The
women's dresses consisted chiefly of loose white
sacques, without the cumbrous under-layer of
petticoats, or the other "troublesome disguises"
that Europe conceals her beauties withal; and they
reserved their assortment of bright but rarely
inharmonious colours for their fantastic turbans,
some of which were arranged so as to give the
effect of one or two moderate-sized horns pro-
jecting from the wearer's head, while other girls,
with better taste, left an embroidered end hang-
ing down on one side, Eastern fashion. Many of
the women were handsome, shapely figures, full-
limbed, and full-bosomed; but—must I say it?—
the particular charm of delicate feet and hands
was universally wanting; nor, indeed, could it
have been fairly looked for among a throng of
field-labourers, female or male. As to faces, the
peculiarities of the negro countenance are well
known in caricature; but a truer pattern may be
seen, by those who wish to study it, any day
among the statues of the Egyptian rooms in the
British Museum: the large gentle eye, the full
but not over-protruding lips, the rounded contour,

and the good-natured, easy, sensuous expression.
This is the genuine African model—one not often,
I am aware, to be met with in European or
American thoroughfares, where the plastic African
too readily acquires the careful look and even
the irregularity of the features that surround him,
but which is common enough in the villages and
fields where he dwells after his own fashion,
among his people; most common of all in the
tranquil seclusion and congenial climate of a
Surinam plantation. There you may find, also, a
type neither Asiatic nor European, but distinctly
African ; with much of independence and vigour
in the male physiognomy, and something that
approaches, if it does not quite reach, beauty in
the female. Rameses and his Queen were cast in
no other mould.*

The Governor and ourselves were seated, with
becoming dignity, on the wide open balcony atop
of the steps leading up to the hall-door, thus com-
manding a full view of the garden and the people

* I am glad that so keen and so discriminating an observer as
the late Mr. Winwood Reade concurs with this very opinion ;
in support of which he cites the authority of Livingstone himself. *Vide* ' African Sketch Book,' vol. i. page 108.

assembled. Immediately in front of us was a large flower-bed, or rather a labyrinth of flower-beds, among which stood, like white goblins in the moonlight, the quaint statues before mentioned, methodically arranged after the most approved Dutch style, and flanked by two pieces of mimic artillery. Such was the centre-piece, and on either side there opened out a wide, clear space, clean swept, and strewn with "caddy," the usual white mixture of broken shell, coral, and sand, and in each of these spaces to right and left a band of musicians, or rather noise-makers, squatted negro-wise on the ground. Round these centres of attraction the crowd soon gathered in a double group, men and women, all noisy, animated, and ready for the dance. The moon, almost at the full, glittered bright overhead; and her uncertain light, while giving full effect to the half-barbaric picturesqueness of attire and form in the shifting eddy of white-clad figures, served also to veil from too exact view the defects (and they were many) in the clothes, ornaments, and appearance of the performers. Around the garden, and behind it, dark masses of palm, almond-tree, acacia, "saman," and kindred growths rose

against the sky, loftier and denser in seeming
than by day; the whole formed an oval picture
of brightness and life, amid a dark and silent
framework of shadow—a scene part gay, part
impressive, and very tropical above all.

The music, or what did duty for such, began.
At first it was of a European character, or, rather,
travestied from European—disintegrated quad-
rilles and waltzes to no particular time. The negroes
around, shy as they always are when in the presence
of those whose criticisms they fear—for no race is
more keenly sensitive in regard to ridicule than
the African, except it be perhaps the semi-African
Arab—did not at once venture to put forth all
their prowess, and the performance opened with
a few sporadic couples, women dancing with
women, men pousseting to men, and either seeming half ashamed of their own audacity. But as
the music continued and grew livelier, passing
more and more from the imitation European to
the unfeigned African style of an unbroken
monotonous drone, with one ever-recurring ca-
dence—a mere continuity of clanging sound—the
dancers grew more animated; new couples, in
which the proper interchange of sex was observed

by the partners, formed themselves; till at last
the larger group, that on our left, took up the
genuine Ethiopian dance, well known in Oman,
and witnessed by me there and elsewhere in the
pleasant days, now long since gathered to the
ineffectual past, when the East and I were one.
A dance of life, where men ranged on one side,
and women on the other, advance, retreat, cross,
join hands, break into whirling knots of twos and
fours, separate, re-form in line, to blend again
into a seeming maze of orderly confusion—a
whirl of very madness, yet with method in it;
the intoxication of movement and sound, poured
out in time and measure. He who has witnessed
it, if there yet flow within his veins one drop of
that primal savage blood, without which man-
kind, and womanhood too, are not much better
than mere titular names, cannot but yield himself up to the influence of the hour, cannot but
drink of the bowl, join in the revel: and if any
looker-on retains coolness enough to sneer or
blame—why, let each follow his bent; but I, for
one, had rather be on the side of David than of
Michal; and the former had, in the end, I think,
the best of the jest, and of the earnest too.

But it is a different thing with those who, amid
the decorous surroundings of a European drawing-room, read, paper-cutter in hand, of what
they have never experienced; and many a fair
woman, and even a brave man, may be a very
Michal in spirit to the narrative, who might have
been of a different mind if some power had taken
them up and set them down again in the flesh
amid the moonlight gardens by the Cottica river
and Munnickendam. And, therefore, of what
was said or done by his Excellency the Governor,
or by his ex-Oriental or ex-Egyptian associates,
and the other non-Ethiopian beholders of the
dance, I will hold my peace; and if all or any
of them cast aside the part of critical spectator
for that of impassioned partner, if any official of
high Batavian rank and dignity forgot, in the un-
veiled arms—I say no more—of his light-robed,
lithe-limbed, though dark-skinned partner, the
tight-buttoned, gold-laced uniform in the ward-
robe at home,—if any guest who had, once on a
time, drunk deep—too deeply, perhaps—of the
waters of the Egyptian Nile re-enacted, or at
least revived, the memories of its shores on the
banks of the South-American river,—the folly or

the wisdom was theirs, and theirs it may remain
in story, as in fact, for me.

A Bacchanalian orgie, yet one in which
Bacchus himself had no share : Venus alone presided, and sufficed for all beside ; or if Bacchus
seemed present to her aid, it was not he, but
Cupid in disguise. Half an hour—an hour—the
revelry continued, while the tumult grew every
minute louder, and the dance more vehement;
till, with an impulse simultaneous in its sudden-
ness, the double chorus broke up, and, blending
in one confused mass, surrounded his Excellency
the Governor, while, amid shouts, laughter, and
huzzas, half-a-dozen sturdy blacks caught him up
in their arms and bore him aloft in triumphal
procession three times round the garden, while
others gesticulated and pressed alongside; others
danced before, all cheered, and we ourselves,
aroused from our Africano-Oriental dream by the
local significance of the act, hardly knew whether
to laugh at or to yield to the enthusiasm of the
moment. That the Governor, though maintaining, as far possible, an appearance of passive
dignity and deprecatory acquiescence, heartily
enjoyed the spontaneous tribute of affection and

loyalty thus tumultuously expressed, I have no
doubt; and so would you have enjoyed it, my
dear reader, had it been offered you. Besides,
he told me as much when, after a tremendous
outburst of huzzas, his living throne gently dis-
solved asunder, and allowed him footing on the
ground again.

And what if in the next-enacted pantomime
there was less of national or personal loyalty in
its impulse, less of subject deference in its manner?
To be enthroned, entwined in the rounded arms,
and borne aloft on the shapely shoulders of six
buxom, laughing damsels, and so carried in a
thrice-repeated circle of unsolicited and un-
expected triumph, while a whole troup of African
sister-beauty danced and cheered around, was a
dignity that left him on whom it was conferred
nothing to envy in the honours bestowed on the
august representative of Dutch royalty himself.
But on whom that happiness was lavished, why it
was so lavished, how received, how requited—
though favours like these are, I allow, beyond all
equipoise of requital—I have once more nothing
to say; whoever would know, let him take sail or
oar up stream to Munnickendam, and inquire there.

Then after a half-hour's pause, congratulations exchanged, healths drunk, and cordial merriment, in which all shared alike, performers, spectators, Europeans, negroes, and the rest, once more to the dance, but now in calmer measure and to a gentler tune. By this the moon, small and dazzling, rode high in the purple heavens, giving warning of midnight near; when escorted down to the water's edge by those whose sports we had witnessed, and perhaps in part shared, we reluctantly threaded the dark shades of the avenue riverwards, and re-embarked on our little steamer that had yet to bear us a mile further along the current before we reached the night's lodging and rest prepared for us by the District Magistrate, in his large and comfortable residence at Ephrata, —so the place was called.

"I wished you to see something of our black creoles as they are among themselves," said the Governor, as next morning we pursued our downward way to the river junction at the Sommelsdyk Fort, and thence turned off southward to explore the upper branch of the Commeweyne, which we had on our way up passed by unvisited. Deep black, and much more rapid than the Cottica, its current flowed between noble forest-scenes, alternating with cultivated spaces on either bank; but few large sugar estates came in view: plantains, cocoa-nuts, cassava, with cocoa bushes intermixed, seemed the more favourite growths. The yearly amount of sugar manufactured in this district does not exceed 1,000 hogsheads; the mills are all of the simplest kind, and moved by water-power. In general character, the scenery and waterside objects of the Upper Commeweyne nearly resemble those of the Upper Cottica, and have been sufficiently described before; a gradual diminution of underwood, an increase of height and girth in the forest trees, and a greater variety in them and in the flowering creepers that inter-lace their boughs, being for many miles up country almost the only distinct indications of approach to the higher lands beyond; though the practised eye of a naturalist might doubtless detect many significant varieties in the insects or plants of the region. These things have their interest, their value too; and who has eyes to see them—a Wallace, a Bates, a Darwin,—let him see: my narrower range of vision, limited alike by ignorance and habit, reaches little further than to

the ways and conditions of the human inhabitants,
their works and pleasures, progress or decay. No
great matters in themselves, it may be; but every
man is a link in the chain of conscious intelligence,
that binds in one the universe of time and space;
and the least result, however capricious seeming,
of thought and will has a wider and more
durable meaning than the vastest and most
regular development of blind unknowing force.
Thought underlies that too, but hidden in depths
we cannot reach; in man alone it rises to the
surface, and to study it there best befits surface-
minds, and of these mine is one.

And now as we slowly stem the liquid glass,
black as jet, yet pure as crystal, of the strong-
flowing Commeweyne, we remark, the Governor
and I, the evident and recent increase in the
number of small plantations, to the detriment,
though a temporary one only, if events run their
regular course, of the larger properties. This is
a necessary phase of free labour, and through it
the Surinam colony, like every other of like kind,
must pass before it can reach the firm ground of
self-sustaining prosperity. Till then nothing is
solid, nothing sure. Giant sugar estates, propped

up or absolutely maintained by extraneous capital,
and excluding, or dwarfing into comparative
nullity, the varied parcel-cultivation of local
ownership and resources, are at best magnificent
gambling speculations; most so when the price
of their produce is not stored up, but at once
applied to widening the enclosures, or purchasing
some costly refinements of improved machinery.
Establishments like these are every instant at the
mercy of a sudden fluctuation of the market, of
a new invention, of a tariff; in a word, they lie
exposed to every accident of Fortune's caprice;
and, capricious as she is throughout her whole
domain, nowhere is the goddess more so than in
the commercial province. Hence it follows that
they who repine at the lengthening catalogue of
five-acre and ten-acre lots, railing at their cultiva-
tors as idle pumpkin-eating squatters, and raising
a desponding moan, occasionally an indignant
howl, over the consequent withdrawal of labour
from the five-hundred or thousand acre estates,
are not more reasonable in their complaints than
he who should fall foul of the workmen employed
in digging and laying the foundations of the
house, and declare them to be lazy loons, and

their labour valueless, because they do not at once bestow it on raising the second story and furnishing the drawing-room. Patience awhile: these things will come in course; but, if the foundation be not first strongly laid, how about the security of the upper stories? — if there be no larder and cellar, what will avail the handsome but sterile furniture of the drawing-room?

Self-interest reasonably pursued is the best interest, not of self only, but of all others besides; and while we admit that the negro small proprietor may very possibly have no one's benefit immediately in view but his own, we must not conclude that he is, by that same reason, less efficaciously assuring the benefit of others. He is in very fact assuring it much more efficaciously and lastingly than if he had hired himself out as day-labourer at the lowest imaginable wages on the biggest sugar estate of the colony.

In Dutch Guiana, taking Paramaribo, the capital, for its centre, we may regard the rest of the territory as made up, after a rough fashion, of three concentric circles. The circumference of the innermost one would, for what concerns the east and the districts we have now been visiting,

pass through the confluence-point of the Commeweyne and Cottica rivers at Sommelsdyk Fort; the
second would intersect through the estate of
" La Paix," on the Upper Cottica, and the corresponding estate of " Abendsrust," on the Upper
Commeweyne; the external limits of the third
would be correlative with those of the colonial
frontier itself. Within the first circle, large
estates, mostly owned by Europeans, or at any
rate European creoles, predominate. Throughout
the second or intermediate circle, smaller properties, mostly in the hands of coloured or black
creoles, are more common. In the outermost
space are the villages and provision-grounds, few
and far between, of the Bush negroes, between
whom and the European landholders the dark
creoles thus form a sort of link, social as well as
territorial, or, to vary the phrase, a connecting
medium, destined, if our conjectures be true, to
become ultimately an absorbing one, not only
of the more savage, but of the more civilized
element also.

But we are forgetting his Excellency. " In
the labourers of Munnickendam," he continued,
" you have a fair sample of our black creoles.

Throughout the colony they are everywhere essentially the same,—fond enough, as you have seen, of pleasure and amusement when they can get them, but when at work steady, sober, willing, and, which is a fortunate thing for all parties, without a trace of social or political restlessness in any direction. Their only fault is that there is not enough of them; and, what is worse, their numbers do not increase."

Why not? Unhealthy climate, some will say; while others, in concert with a late author, talk in bated breath of gross and ruinous vices, rendering it a question whether negroes should exist on the earth at all for a few generations longer; and others again find in infanticide a third and convenient solution of the question. Let us look a little closer.

And, first, for the climate. Like British Guiana, its Dutch namesake is a low-lying plain, swampy in some places, forest-grown in others, and far within the tropics—none of them at first sight favourable conditions to salubrity of atmosphere. But where fresh sea-winds sweep over the earth day and night, with scarcely interrupted steadiness from year's end to year's end,

an open plain is healthier by far than the
sheltered valleys and picturesque nooks of a
mountainous district; and, among tidal streams
on a tidal coast, the marsh-fevers, that render the
moist shores of the stagnant Black Sea pool
scarcely less pestilential than those of Lagos itself,
find little place. Tropical heat, though here it is
never excessive, does not, certainly, in the long
run suit European residents; and at Surinam,
where 79° Fahr. is the yearly average, the
highest ever recorded being 96° Fahr., and the
lowest 70°, the climate must be admitted to be a
warm one. On the other hand, those who have
experience of Africa, the negroes' birthplace, or
have seen how much the black suffers in the comparatively moderate chill of winter-season in the
northern West Indian Islands, will hardly consider the heat of Dutch Guiana to be too great
for the species that forms a good four-fifths of its
population.

As to the second-named cause, or collection
of causes rather, it is to be regretted that the
author of 'At Last' should, from ignorance
doubtless, or prejudice, have ever lent such vague
and baseless calumnies the sanction of his

respected name. Without being either a "clergy-
man" or even, though an official, a "police
magistrate," I have knowledge enough of negro
character and ways to warrant me in asserting,
and my readers in believing the assertion, that
what is technically called vice is among Africans
nearer allied to philoprogenitiveness than among,
it may well be, most other races. And without
attempting to excuse, much less—as some seem
inclined to do—to vindicate, the extreme laxity of
their theory and practice in regard of connubial
fidelity or maiden virtue, one must allow that
their faults in these respects tend much more
directly to the increase of the population than to
its diminution. And to have done once for all
with a topic, the mention of which, though
unavoidable, is unpleasing, it may here be
added, that excess in alcoholic drink—a fault
decidedly opposed, as all who have studied the
subject know, to the "increase and multiply"
of healthy nature—is rare among the black
creoles of the Surinam capital, and rarer still,
indeed almost unknown, among those of the
country. So much for the second cause assigned.

A mere inspection of the yearly birth-rate, averaging thirty per 1,000, disposes of the third allegation. Murdered children are not entered on parochial registers, nor do the numbers given leave much margin for kindred crimes at an earlier stage.

And yet the annual death-rate exceeds that of births by at least one per cent., as is stated, and this at the best of times. Some years show two per cent., or even higher. How is this? And if neither climate, nor vice, nor crime be the cause, where is it then to be sought?

But here let some indulgence be asked and given. We are on board a pleasure boat; and our attention is being called away every moment, now to gaze on a " tall tree by the side of the river, one half of which was in flames," or rather flowers red as flames, and not less bright, " from the root to the top, and the other half green and in full leaf," that might have reminded Geraint and Enid of their Celtic wonderland; now to acknowledge the shouted welcome of bright figures crowding to some little landing-place on the way; now by an opening vista of glittering plantain groves, now by a tray full of glasses

P

with appropriate contents, circulating at frequent intervals round the deck. Amid interruptions like these, it must be admitted that profound investigations, statistical columns, and a marshalled array of figures and facts would be hardly less out of place than a sermon at a masked ball. But it is possible to say truth, and even serious truth, without sermonizing—*ridentem dicere vera*, and the rest; we will try.

All have heard, and all who have not merely heard but seen will attest, the fondness of negroes for children; nor their own children only, but any, white, brown, or black,—for children generically taken, in a word. Demonstrative as is their affection, it is none the less genuine; the feeling is instinctive, and the instinct itself is hardly ever absent from among them. I do not put it forward as a matter of praise; I mention it as a fact. If Sir S. Baker's sweeping assertion regarding I forget how many negro tribes, that they have among them no acknowledged form of worship of the Unknown, were exact, which it is not, the existence, the universality, indeed, of baby-worship, at any rate, must be allowed, I think, even by that distinguished

miso-African. Nor is this species of worship
limited to the mothers of the babies, or to the
womankind at large; it is practised in the same
degree by the men, who are not a whit behind
the women in their love and care of children,
especially the youngest.

But, unfortunately, just as men of all tribes
and ages invariably make their gods after their
own image and likeness, so also they worship
them after their own fashion, and within the
limits of their own habits and ways. Now
negroes, and—I beg the ladies' pardon, but truth
is truth, and must be told—negresses still more,
are essentially irreflective; keen-visioned enough
for the immediate present, consequences are as
nothing in their sight. The "In-sha-Allah,"
"Allah-Kereem," "Ala-bab-Illah," and so forth,
of the Arab, but half express the "happy-go-
lucky" habit of mind of his African cousin.
And so it comes about that, in the very fervour
and ecstasy of her baby-worship, the negress-
mother persists in worshipping her little divinity
irreflectively, recklessly, and, by a natural consequence, often injuriously, sometimes destruc-
tively, to the baby-god itself.

Heated from field-work, excited, overdone, she returns in the late afternoon to her cottage; and the first thing she does when arrived there is to catch up her little brown sprawler from the floor, and put it to her breast. The result needs no guessing. Half an hour later she is howling as only a negress can howl over her offspring, convulsed or dead. Or, perhaps, just as she was about to give, in more orderly fashion, the nourishment that the infant has been faintly wailing after for some time past, a friend comes in to invite her to a dance or merry-making close by. Off she goes, having made Heaven knows what arrangements for the small creature's wants, or it may well be, in her eagerness for amusement, no arrangement at all; purposes to come back in an hour, stays away until midnight, and, on her return home, finds another midnight, the midnight that knows no sunrise, closed over her child. And thus, and more. On over-feeding, injudicious feeding, ailments misunderstood, quack-doctoring, always preferred by the ignorant to all other,—on half-superstitious usages not less injurious than silly,—on violent outbursts of passion—the passions of a negress, and of a negro, too, are at tropical heat, their rage absolute frenzy,—I need not dwell; suppose what you will, you will be short of the mark. But cease to wonder if, among the most kindly hearted, child-loving, and, I may add, child-producing race in the world, births, however numerous, are less in computation than deaths; if one-third at least by statistical registration, one full half, if to its records be added the unregistered fact, of the negro children in Dutch Guiana die even before they are weaned. The causes, ninety-nine out of a hundred, are those which I have stated or alluded to, and no other.

What is then to be done? An evil, or, rather, an agglomeration of evils like these, that threaten to cut down the main-stem of the future, to dry up the very roots, to destroy the existence of the colony, must be put an end to, all will agree; but how?

"Educate the mothers." Excellent! try it. Education, even among races already at a much higher level of culture than the Guiana negro, is not a thing of a day; no, nor of a generation either. Look at home, and say how much has the omnipotence of an Act of Parliament done to perfect it, even among "the heirs of all the ages," among ourselves.

Educate: yes, by all means; but if this, my intelligent European friend, be your sole remedy, you will find its application made easy enough, but by a process on which you have not calculated— the process of extinction. For long before the slow-working panacea has so much as begun to exercise its beneficial effects—before the first lessons are well learnt, the first prizes awarded— the number of your scholars will be so few that a child may write them, if, indeed, there are any children left to write.

Well, then, medical supervision, and that immediate, say you. Of the medical staff of the colony, its efficiency and its defects also, I shall have occasion to say something in the next chapter. But in suggesting it in the present instance you have shown yourself to be merely a bachelor, and a theoretical bachelor, too. The infant field is one in which, for every square foot of doctor's ground, whole acres belong to the mother and the nurse—a territory into which the M.D. is not often or willingly called, even by those who understand his value, hardly ever by those who do not. Did Dutch Guiana possess twenty times more doctors than are now within her limits, and were each one of them twenty times as efficacious in his craft, all their learning and skill would go for little in this matter, do as they might: the evil lies far away, the most part beyond their reach.

Must, then, this waste of life continue unchecked? Is no remedy to be found? There is a remedy, and a very simple one; tried before, and worth trying again. Let us go back in memory to the times when every individual negro life meant so many hundred florins to his owner; when the suppression of the "trade" had cut off the supply from without, and the birth of every slave-child on the estate brought a clear gain to the planter, just as its death represented an actual and heavy loss hard to replace, not to the parents only, but to the owner of parents and children, too. Negroes and negresses might be never so unthinking then—never so reckless about what concerned themselves alone; but their master took good thought that they should not be careless where his own interest was involved. And in few things was it so closely involved, especially after the treaties of 1815 and 1819, as in the preservation of infant life among the labouring stock ; and no precaution was neglected that could insure this, and supplement the defects of maternal care.

Many means were adopted, but the chiefest of all was the appointment, on every estate, of one or more of elderly women, appropriately styled "mammas," chosen from among the negresses themselves, and whose sole duty was to watch each over a given number of infantile negroes, for whose proper care, nourishment, and good condition generally this foster-mother had to answer, and for whose loss, if they drooped and died, she was called to strict account.

The history of slave institutions has been not inappropriately called the "devil's book"; but here, at any rate, is a leaf of it worth taking out for insertion in a better volume. This could easily be done in Surinam. The colony is, from old time, divided into districts, eleven in all, the capital included ; and over these, though not in exact correspondence with their number and limits, are set medical officers, appointed by Government, and charged to see to the public health, and that of the labouring classes in particular. Now my suggestion would be this: Let there be appointed to each district, not a doctor or surgeon only, but "negro mammas," middle-aged women, one or more according to the local requirements, whose duty would be to keep and render account of all the black or coloured children born on the lands, from two years old and downwards, like the babes of Bethlehem, but with opposite intent. To fit them for their charge, these district nurses, to give them a more civilized-sounding name than that borne by their predecessors of old days, should have received sufficient instruction, both in the causes and characters of infantile ailments, and in the right manner of their treatment, so that they might be able of themselves to deal with ordinary cases, and, in general, to prescribe and regulate, when needed, the nourishment and care necessary for maintaining good health among the little folks. They should also be obliged to keep an exact register of every birth, and a list of all the children under their charge, and from time to time, say once a month, they should be called on to report to the medical officer of their district, to whom, and through him to the Government, they should be responsible within the limits of their district, for the well or ill being, the health, sickness, or death, of those entrusted to them. In a word, they should do for the free-born infants as much, or rather more, and that after a better regulated and more intelligent fashion, than was done on the slave-estates of the pre-emancipation era.

Now, fill up this outline-project with the proper colouring of qualifications, provisoes, regulations, and the remaining supplemental details of theory wrought out into fact, and you will have a scheme for the preservation of infant negro life, or rather the hindrance of its prodigal and ruinous waste, more likely to succeed in its object than any that I have yet heard or seen in practice. Then combine these or similar measures with a reasonable supply of the two needful things, without which neither Surinam nor any other trans-Atlantic colony can prosper or, indeed, exist—capital and immigration. Not the capital of official subsidy, but of private enterprise; nor the immigration of costly and burdensome East-Indian coolies, or the yet costlier and yet more

troublesome Chinese, but of vigorous, healthy,
willing East Africans, the ex-slaves of the
Zanzibar and Oman markets. Then put these
three requisites together, and stand up and pro-
phesy to Dutch Guiana what golden-aged future
you will, nor fear being numbered in the latter
days among the false prophets; your place will be
with the true. This done, spread the gilding of
education wide and thick as you please, but first
secure the mass to spread it on withal. Is not the
life more than meat, even school meat? and the
body more than raiment, even the raiment of
knowledge, were it gorgeous as that of Solomon
himself?

The sea ebb has set the dammed-up waters of
the Commeweyne at liberty to follow their
natural bent, and we float swiftly down the
stream, admiring, commenting, and enjoying,
now the ever-varying, ever-recurring scenes of
life and labour of tropical nature and European
energy, of forest, plantation, mansion, cottage,
and field that every river-bend unfolds; now the
"feast of reason and the flow of soul,"—a very
hackneyed phrase,—as we go; and now more substantial feastings, and the flow of various compo-

sitions very congenial to the Dutch soul and body too, nor less so to the English. But the distance was considerable, and night looked down on us with its thousand starry eyes long before we reached Fort Amsterdam and the broad Surinam waters. An hour later, we disembarked at the Government " Stelling " of the silent capital, well pleased with our river excursion and with each other also.

Not many days after, I was riding out with the Governor on the high road,—that is to say, on the horse-path, for the true high road here, as elsewhere in Guiana, is by water,—leading towards the wooded regions of Para, south-west of Paramaribo, to which, in composition with some other Indian word, it has given its name. Its inhabitants are reckoned, exclusive of Bush negroes, at nearly 5,000. They live in villages, and occupy themselves, to some extent, in sugar-cultivation, but, generally, in small lots, where they grow cocoa, coffee, and plantains. Indigo and tobacco are also among the products of the land. The ground is well raised above the water-level; to the south, indeed, it becomes hilly. The forest scenery is said to surpass in beauty, as in extent, that of any other district in the colony. "You can ride for seven days in one direction, without ever getting out of the shade," said the Governor, as I noticed the noble outskirts of the woods before us ; and he urged on me, almost as a duty, a visit to Para, where, amid the small creole proprietors and the forest-embowered villages, he assured me I should see Surinam negro life to better advantage, witness greater comfort and contentment, act as spectator or sharer, if the fancy took, of gayer festivities, than even on the banks of the Cottica and at Munnickendam. But my hank of Surinam thread was too nearly spun out already ; and the colours of other lands were now about to take its place in the fate-woven twine.

CHAPTER VII.

THE COLONY.

" It would be interesting to know the secret of Dutch colonial management, wh'ch presents to an outside observer the aspect of minding one's own business, and inducing other people to mind theirs."—*Saturday Review.*

THREE mottoes head this work.   The first has its embodiment in the descriptions given, or at least attempted, of places and people.   The third assigns the tone of the mental colouring thrown by the seer himself over what he saw.   But the second motto is chiefly referable to the summing up; it is a conjecture, the verification of which, if it has the good luck to be verified, must be sought in the conclusion.   And this is why I have recalled it to eye and mind at the head of this, the concluding chapter.

Either my narrative has been very inadequate to its subject, or the reader very inattentive, if he has not long ago drawn two distinct and, in some degree, opposite inferences from the preceding chapters: one, that Surinam is not, in a progressive or money-making sense, a very prosperous colony; the other, that it is, on the whole, a remarkably well managed one. But how far its good management may be due to the workings of the twofold secret suggested by the critic, whose clever conjecture I have quoted, is not equally self-evident. "The former," *i.e.*, minding one's own business, is, he subjoins, "usually not easy"; "the latter," *i.e.*, inducing other people to mind theirs, "generally impracticable." If so, all the more credit to those who have compassed them in act. Whether the Dutch lords of Surinam have really done so will, I think, become more apparent on a general though foreshortened view of the colony as a whole.

The beginnings of Dutch Guiana were those of a mere settlement. When early in 1667 the Zeelander, Admiral Krynnsen, with three ships and 600 soldiers, wrested the land from its English occupants, he made it over, in right of government as of property, to the particular State whence he had received his commission and equipment, and by which he was himself, under the title of "Commander," appointed Governor of the territory that he had conquered. His adminstration was wholly military, and the settlers had to accept the rule, no less than the protection, of the garrison and the fleet. A few years later the States General of Holland claimed for themselves the right of nominating the Governor of Surinam; and shortly after the State of Zeeland, dissatisfied with the financial results of its enterprise, sold its territorial right, partly to the Dutch West-Indian Company of those days, partly to the city of Amsterdam. But, however much the external relations of the settlement were modified by these changes, its internal management remained the same; and military rule, unchecked by law, was fast degenerating into mere anarchical tyranny, when the appointment as Governor of the Count of Sommelsdyk not only saved the settlement from disintegration and ruin, but gave it an entirely new and durable character.

In fact, the existence of the colony as such may truly be said to date from the 24th of November, 1683, when this large-minded and high-spirited man landed at Paramaribo. A cursory notice has already been taken of the principal events that marked his short but brilliant administration. To it and him the colony owes its two main institutions, the Council of Policy and the Court of Justice. Indeed, during the whole of the eighteenth and a portion of the nineteenth century, constant struggles with foreign hostilities —chiefly French—from without, and within servile revolts, followed by stranger-occupation and financial difficulties of the most serious kind, left small leisure for administrative development, and, till a comparatively recent date, the Governor, with the two courts already mentioned, summed up in themselves almost the entire programme of colonial management. But the eight-fold district division introduced in 1842 gave new elasticity to the administration, and this important measure was followed by a series of improvements in every department, that have rendered the machinery of the Government almost as complete in detail as comprehensive in plan.

What, then, is the actual administration of the colony? and, first of all, on what basis is it reared? What is the ground-plan of the simple yet multiple structure that covers and protects the land? And let us not be surprised, much less offended, if it is not entirely in accord with

Q

our own political conceptions : there is always something to be learned from those who disagree with us; rarely from those who agree.

King, Lords, and Commons, a triple machine, with each part equibalanced in the correctest imaginable counterpoise,—such is, in the main, the English constitutional ideal of a government as it should be. On the other hand, caste rule, however disguised, is hardly less generally admitted to be the ideal of a government as it should not be. Both these estimates are, we may safely assert, tolerably correct, where empires of wide extent, and nations that have already attained an advanced degree of development, are concerned; but it does not follow that both or either should be absolute, indisputable truth for all places, at all times, and under all conditions. Systems are very satisfactory things to those who devise them; their only inconvenience is that, when they come to be applied, they are so rarely commensurate with realities. Procrustes doubtless found his bed answer to perfection the purposes for which he designed it; but it is doubtful whether its occupants were generally of the same opinion.

That a certain West-Indian island—I think,

St. Lucia—then on the point of receiving the
blessings of a constitution might get as much as
possible of the Queen or King, and as little as
possible of the Lords and Commons, was the
sensible wish of the very sensible Anthony Trollope, when visiting the Caribbean Archipelago
some twenty-five years since. Now Dutch
Guiana, though geographically part of a very
respectable continent, is to all administrative,
legislative, and social purposes just as much of an
island as St. Lucia itself; and what has been, and
rightly, said of the one, may, for these matters,
be not less rightly said of the other.

How they have ultimately settled it in St. Lucia
I do not know; but in Surinam, at least, the
constitution is almost entirely King. The Governor,
who holds his appointment direct from the Crown,
and to it alone is responsible, through the Colonial
Office at the Hague, to which he has to make a
tri-monthly report of his proceedings, is, within
the common limits of law, almost absolute ruler,
so far as the colony itself is concerned. All local
appointments, all subordinate posts, are in his gift;
he is, by virtue of his office, commander-general
of all garrison troops whatever, by land or sea;

Q 2

every financial measure is subject to his control; the entire administration centres in his person. So much—a lion's share, truly—for the Crown.

Follow Lords and Commons, or, rather, an amalgamation of both ; but their joint share, when compared with the foregoing, shows off modest indeed. Till lately, they were "represented" vaguely enough by a council called "Colonial," which was convoked by the Governor, but solely when he thought fit, and then even merely for consultation and advice. In this council the Governor presided, and, with the "Procureur-General," an official inferior in colonial rank and influence only to the Governor himself, the Finance Administrator, and the Colonial Secretary, made up the *ex-officio* element of the Assembly. The non-official consisted of six Crown members, chosen by the Governor himself from among the most respectable landowners in the colony, or their resident agents. To these six was also entrusted the subordinate administration of the eight districts, some singly, some united, into which the Surinam territory was divided, Coronie and Nickerie excepted—these two being allowed separate magistracies of their own.

The council had, accordingly, a double character : consultative in its corporate capacity, it was
executive in the individuals who composed it ;
while under either aspect it might be not unfairly
regarded as an extension of the Governor's own
personality—little more. It was a Crown aris-
tocracy, with, we may suppose, the customary
advantages and drawbacks of such, modified by
the national type. The " Commons," that is, the
bulk of the population, had, on this plan, neither
voice nor expression in the administration ; nor,
indeed, previous to emancipation and its correlative extension of civic rights, did they require
any.

Yet, even in those days, the government of
Surinam was not an arbitrary one, far from it.
The Colonial Office at the Hague, to which the
Governor was obliged to refer everything, and
from which all his authority derived, acted as one
check. Another existed in the law courts, civil
and criminal, over neither of which had he any
control. A third was ever present at his side in
the person of the " Procureur-General," a nominee
of the Hague, and invested with magisterial
and even political powers hardly inferior to his

own. A fourth was provided in the " Finance-Administrator," whose concurrence in every measure involving serious expenditure was indispensable. With so many restraints, the government was, it is clear, more likely to err on the side of over-caution than of precipitancy or despotism.

When, however, emancipation had, in 1863, converted the bulk of the population into Dutch citizens, without distinction of colour or caste, some corresponding change became necessary, if not in the essentials, at least in the form of administration. This was done by creating a House of Assembly, where the Governor takes his seat as President, supported by four official or Crown members, nominated by himself, and nine other members, elected by voters, and holding their seats each for six years. Vacancies occasioned by death, retirement, or the course of rotation are filled up by general election; a yearly payment of taxes to the amount of forty florins constitutes a voter. The power of the Assembly is limited to debating on measures submitted to its consideration by the Governor, who is not bound by their opinion, unless, indeed, it coincides

with his own, in which case the measure becomes
law, subject always to approval and confirmation
from the Hague. The Assembly has no initiative
power, nor any direct financial control. Should
the Governor find it advisable to act in opposition
to the majority of the members, he can do so ;
but he is bound to supply the dissentients with a
written explanation of his motives, with which
they are similarly bound to be satisfied, and there
ends the matter.

The Assembly is, in fact, nothing but the old
deliberative council under another shape, with a
decorous flavour of the " Commons," so introduced that they too, on condition of their remaining in accordance with the Governor, may bear a
part in the dignity of administration; otherwise
they are practically excluded from it. Meanwhile, the creation of seven district commissaries,
the Governor's own nominees, between whom the
executive sub-management of the entire Surinam
territory, from frontier to frontier, is portioned
out, while an eighth, as burgomaster, has in
charge the capital itself, takes away from the
" Assembly " every remnant of the administrative
character supported by the " council " of former

days. This has been transferred, within certain limits, to the new "Advising" or "Privy" Council, another phase of the old one, but on a narrower scale, since it now includes three persons only—the Governor, the Colonial Secretary, the " Procureur-General," and three other members, selected by the Governor, and nominated by the King. From all which it results that the Governor's hands are, to practical purposes, about as much and as little tied as formerly ; nor has the relative official position of King, Lords, and Commons been substantially changed in Dutch Guiana by or since the constitution of the " Assembly " in 1865. Summing up, King, in his own person or those of the Colonial Minister and the Governor, almost everything; Lords, in a consultative capacity, something; Commons, honorary ;—such is the government of Surinam.

Or, rather, so is Surinam governed :—passive, not active. The colonial administration is a portion of the home machinery, and obeys the same central force ; not a distinct engine working apart.

A system like this has its drawbacks; what system has not ? It has also its advantages, and they are many. Against the absence of spontaneity, it has for set-off the assurance of security. One thing deserves especial notice : it is that, under an administration thus constituted, diversity of colour and race can be safely, as occasion requires, disregarded in the colony ; which could never be the case did the officials derive their nomination and powers from the colony itself. White, black, or coloured, all are subjects alike—all equally dependent on an authority beyond the seas; and where such is the common footing, caste-feeling has, it will be admitted, little or nothing to encourage it in the distribution of nominations, towards which its influence has in nowise contributed. Nor are factions likely to quarrel for the decorations of official power or the sweets of official perquisites, nor even to exist at all, where the control of these desirable things is beyond the control of any faction or party whatsoever. Public opinion there certainly is, in Surinam as elsewhere; nor can it be absolutely disregarded with impunity on the banks of the Commeweyne, any more than on those of the Yssel. But public opinion is never more moderate and judicious than when it feels itself to be restricted within the limits of simple opinion, and has no recognized expression in act. Hence the Governor remains free, or nearly so, to select at pleasure the most capable and the best deserving candidates to fill the many posts of office within his gift, throughout the territory, without needing anxiously to consider in every instance what may be the pedigree, or what the epidermal hue, of the individual appointed. Hence, too, the office-holders themselves, unimpeded by party ties, are all tho more likely to devote their entire attention to the satisfactory performance of their duties—a moral impossibility did they owe their position to faction and intrigue. Nor are the good effects confined to the officials themselves; they pervade tho whole population : and the secret of getting every one to mind his own business is thus found to resolve itself into the correlative and not more abstruse secret of giving no one the temptation to mind any one's business except his own.

"A most autocratic style of administration, and one that would not at all go down with us," I hear some colonial Briton—Antiguan, it may be, or Grenadan, or Barbadian—say. To such I have no answer to make : if they are content with themselves and their condition, it is well; and Heaven forbid I should wish them otherwise. But should a like comment be uttered by a friend from Canada, Tasmania, Queensland, Victoria, and so forth, the reply is ready. Remember, then, O Canadian, Tasmanian, or whatever you be, that in colonies, not large like your own, but small, very small, and in the presence, not of a tolerably homogeneous population, but of one in which the vast majority is composed of a race or races inferior, by nature perhaps, perhaps by circumstances actual or antecedent, local self-government involves problems singularly difficult to solve aright. If frankly conceded, it must include all the component members of the colony, and that on an equal footing; if otherwise, it can be nothing but caste rule under a thin disguise. For an example of what the former leads to, take Jamaica from 1836 to 1865 ; for a specimen of the latter, see . . . but I will not particularize. Which do you prefer—the lordship of misrule, or the lordship of Bumbledom? tumultuous anarchy or respectable stagnation ? For to one or the other you must come, according as you follow the former system or the latter, according as you put within the reach

of all, or withhold from some, that most seductive temptation, the temptation of self-rule, after
once displaying it as something attainable before
their eyes. Much better, say I, not to hold it
out at all; and that is just what our Dutch friends
of the Hague have done. "Do you mind your
business," say they to the colonists, " and we will
mind ours. Do you go steadily to work, make the
best you can of the land and its products. Government is our affair, and we will look after it":—a
wise partition of labour, and deserving the praise
not of the Saturday Reviewer only, but of all
reviewers who have ever sat in the censor's chair.

In a word ,party spirit, colour-antagonism, does
not exist in Surinam, because it has never been
summoned by opportunity into existence; and
to its absence we may, in great measure, attribute
the freedom with which intermarriage, climate,
and those occult local influences that subtly, but
powerfully, modify national types do their work
at large in Dutch Guiana, and cast over the entire
population that uniformity of tint and guise of
which I have already spoken in an earlier chapter
of this work.

And now to come to subordinate details,

liberally furnished by the yearly Surinam Blue
Books, but of which few only need be mentioned
here, and that briefly. And, first, the administration of justice : it is in every respect regulated
by Dutch law and custom, and impartially dealt
out to all. The Supreme Courts of Justice, civil
and criminal, sit at Paramaribo ; and to them all
cases of importance have to be referred. In
addition, six district judges, three of whom enjoy
fixed stations, while the three others go on a kind
of circuit, have authority in lesser matters, decide
disputes between masters and men, and inflict
fines or imprisonment, the former not exceeding
the sum of 300 florins, the latter limited to two
months. These district judges are stipendiary
officials, no landowner or trader being allowed to
perform their part ; while, on the other hand,
they themselves are not always members of the
legal profession—a serious defect, and productive
of much inconvenience. Their sentence, too, is,
in the majority of cases, subject to appeal ; and
this circumstance, added their own want of
personal weight, throws back nearly the whole
judicial duty on the central courts. To those
courts, accordingly, almost every case, trifling or

serious, is ultimately referred, from a rap over the head up to deliberate murder, and from a disputed corial to a lawsuit involving the largest estate in Dutch Guiana. Hence delay and inconvenience without end. A "block" at Temple Bar, before it was pulled down, a Waterloo Station booking-rail on an excursion-day, a Covent Garden box-office on a "Patti" night in the season, feebly image forth the habitual condition of these unlucky courts. Worse still for those who have to come before them. I have myself seen in the Paramaribo Jail *détenus* of more than six months, waiting their turn for a sentence the duration of which, when awarded, would probably not exceed six weeks.

This evil, and it is not a trifling one, might best, I think, be remedied by giving the district magistrates power to deal summarily, and without appeal, as justices of the peace, with minor cases of assault, petty larceny, and the like ; at the same time establishing in the districts themselves two or three places of correction, especially destined for carrying out the execution of light sentences, suited to the offences in hand. In a country where intercommunication is easy, and

under a system that can readily provide the
requisite supervision, no serious abuse need be
feared from such an increase in the local magisterial power; or it could soon be remedied, did
it occur. Meanwhile, the work of the central
courts would be reduced by more than half; and
the now-overcrowded prisons of Paramaribo and
Fort Amsterdam proportionately cleared, to the
great advantage of all parties. Labour is too
valuable an article in Surinam to be kept locked
up a day longer than absolutely necessary, whatever the motive.

Another part of the administration that stands
in need, not so much of reform as of re-adjust-
ment, is taxation. A poll-tax, however graduated,
is invariably odious, almost invariably unfair;
and, in the Surinam of the present day, an
anachronism besides. The poll-tax of Dutch
Guiana owed its origin to the peculiar circumstances
of the slave-holding epoch, when the best standard
for regulating the taxation of freemen was undoubtedly the number of bondsmen in their
employ, as a starting-point from which to arrive
at the rough estimate of the incomes to be taxed.
But, with emancipation, this state of things passed

away ; and the old method is evidently inapplicable to the conditions of free labour. A further inconvenience lies in the difficulty of collection. The bulk of those from whom a poll-tax has to be made up is, of course, formed by the lowest and the poorest classes—field-labourers, woodcutters, charcoal-burners, fishermen, and the like—men who rarely frequent Paramaribo, and are not readily noticed when they do. So the tax-gatherer has to hunt after them himself in their haunts, up the rivers of the interior. But in a region like this, with an unlimited background of wild country, what more easy than to forestall the unwelcome official visit by a temporary absence in the bush? Nor, in the absence of the dweller of the hut, does distraining offer much chance of satisfaction where there is generally nothing, except, maybe, a broken bottle, to distrain ; nor demolition, where there is nothing to be demolished that cannot be rebuilt in half a day. So that in every respect the poll-tax is not a success.

Another error is embodied in the colonial export duties, ranging from five to ten per cent. on the value of the goods—an unadvisable source of revenue, because tending directly to the discouragement and disemployment of labour and produce. However, taxation in Surinam, taken altogether, is not over heavy; nor does the burden require so much to be lightened as to be shifted. The fault consists in this, that the strongest shoulders are not under the present system those that have to bear the most load, but the weakest.

I pass lightly over the remaining administrative departments, because they are in general organization identical with those of our own colonies; the differences are slight and of a local character. For these things, see the annual Reports, in which education, charitable institutions, and public works occupy a large space. The statistics of the first show 5,371 children in regular school attendance; a large number, being in fact one-tenth of the entire population, Bush negroes and Indians excepted. About one-half of the schools throughout the colony are maintained by the Moravian Brotherhood, with or without official subsidy, and more than half the remainder by the Government itself. Naturally the education furnished by most of the town schools and

R

by all the country ones is merely elementary.
Among the charitable institutions, a magnificent
hospital, the largest and best appointed I have
seen in the West Indies, a poor-house, also
spacious and well kept, a solidly funded "Bene-
volent" Society, an Orphanage, and the Lepers'
Asylum, at Batavia in the Coronie district,
take the foremost rank. Canals, dams, sluices,
bridges, landing-places, and the other adjuncts of
water-communication are the principal items on
the list of public works. They are maintained,
and from time to time extended, with genuine
Dutch perseverance and skill.

The medical staff of the colony consists of
forty-seven practitioners, apothecaries and mid-
wives included. The police corps, between
officers and men, musters 160 strong. Neither of
these numbers can be considered adequate to the
requirements of so large and so widely scattered
a population. A more numerous and better
organized police force might besides allow the
colony to dispense in great measure with the
expensive services of the over-numerous European garrison, at present maintained for show
rather than use, in the principal forts. Nor need

the good folks of Surinam go any further to look
for the very model and pattern of a police force,
than which none better exists anywhere, than to
their neighbours of Demerara. Lastly, such a
corps, if judiciously blended with the elder institution of "Guides," now for some reason or
another left in abeyance, would prove a useful
instrument for introducing the beginnings of discipline and social order among the Bush negroes,
and thus help to pave the way for the gradual
incorporation of these last into the rest of the
colony.

Sectarian rivalry, a too frequent cause of discord in colonies, whatever their isothermal lines,
has been remarkably innocuous in Surinam,
though not for want of diversity of sects. First
come the Moravians, whose muster-roll runs on
considerably beyond 20,000; next follow Roman
Catholics, who boast about half that number;
only, while the former are chiefly recruited from
among the field-labourers and the negroes, the
latter supply their ranks with a medley of Portuguese, Indians, and arrivals from outside. The
Dutch-Reformed, whose system is, I am told, not
far removed from that of our own Presbyterians,

count only 8,500; but among these are most of the officials and leading men. Their congregation represents, so to speak, the ruling and the burgher element. The peasantry and the land are represented by the Moravian Brotherhood; the lower townsmen and proletarian class, by Roman Catholicism. Lastly, wealth and energy of character bring the Jews, though little over 1,200 in all, to the fore. History, but history only, notices some rather serious bickerings between them and their fellow-colonists; of these and analogous squabbles no trace now remains. Toleration, introduced by the large-mindedness of Van Sommelsdyk, though in the teeth of much opposition and obloquy at the time, has now for two centuries prevailed in principle and in act alike throughout Surinam; nor has any sect had occasion to complain of unfairness in the distribution of official patronage or subsidy. In a word, Government and people have happily agreed in preferring the mellow lotus of dogmatic adiaphorism to the sharp-tasted apple of sectarian discord; may they long abide by their choice. In a field like this, the lotus is the better pasture.

I have made hitherto little mention, and even
that incidental only, of the natural products of
the land, of its wild animals, birds, or insects, of
its trees, plants, fruits, flowers, grasses, and the
rest, because they are in the main identical with
those of British Guiana, and may be found, by
whoever lists, fully catalogued in books descrip-
tive of the latter province. Though ethnogra-
phically divided, the two Guianas—Dutch and
English—are geographically and physically one;
except that a slightly higher elevation above
the sea-level gives to the Dutch moiety of this
region a somewhat healthier climate and a greater
variety of agricultural produce. In the latter
regard, the contrast between Demerara, that land
of sugar and sugar only, and Surinam is certainly
remarkable enough. The yearly statistics of
Demeraran productions are well known; and
though no exact statement, showing the comparative extent of cane land with that appropriated to
other growths, has, to the best of my knowledge,
been published, yet an export list like that of
1873, where, out of a total value of 2,217,432*l.*,
sugar and its twin offspring, molasses and rum,
make up together no less than 2,031,561*l.*, or

almost eleven-twelfths of the whole, sufficiently
indicates the lordship, I had almost said the auto-
cracy, of the cane.

In Surinam it is otherwise. There, indeed,
the painstaking accuracy of Dutch statistics does
not leave us to the complicated and, in a certain
degree, conjectural calculation of the relative proportion between the amount of land laid out in
cane and that allotted to other growths in the
territory. The acres actually under cultivation
in 1873 amounted to 27,817; and of these the
official report for that year assigns 13,646, or
about one-half, to sugar; one-half again of the
remaining land is occupied by cocoa; and the
residual quarter appears as divided between
coffee, cotton, bananas, and the mixed gardening
of provision-grounds.

These proportions have not been always the
same. Thus, for example, cotton, first introduced in 1752, rose into comparative importance
during the English occupation of 1804-16, and
soon secured a sort of monopoly in the Coronie
district, then newly opened to cultivation. In
1832 the number of cotton-growing estates
exceeded sixty : twenty years later it had sunk

to thirty, and of these again seven only have survived down to the present time; five of them are in Coronie, two on the Upper Surinam. Cocoa, the heir-loom of Van Sommelsdyk's administration in 1685, has been more fortunate. For a long time an interloper, and a mere supplementary growth on the spare corners of coffee plantations, it claimed on its own account, even so lately as 1852, only two estates—a number raised in the latest census to thirty-nine, while its produce has absolutely doubled itself within the last five years. On the other hand, coffee, brought hither from Java about the beginning of the eighteenth century, and at one time the main staple of the colony, has steadily dwindled, till, out of 178 plantations registered in 1832, only thirty dragged on a feeble and unproductive existence in 1873. For a diminution like this no satisfactory cause has been assigned; nor can any reason be given why tobacco and indigo, two of the earliest recorded products of the upland of Surinam, should now be represented by a blank in the catalogue of exports.

The extent of the sugar plantations has been already stated. Their number, according to the

latest published surveys, is sixty-five. The
amount of their joint produce exported in 1873,
exceeded in value two millions and a half of
florins. Cocoa furnished half a million more;
cotton somewhat over a hundred thousand; coffee
scarcely found a mention.

Yet, in truth, there is no tropical field-growth
but finds, or might find, a home in Dutch Guiana;
no valuable timber but forms part of her boundless forests; no costly spice is a stranger to her
soil; no useful extract alien from the list of her
resources. Surinam is the triumph of vegetable
life: the triumph of human industry alone is
wanting to subjugate and complete.

Something has certainly been done, and done
well; but how much more remains to do! Out
of a million and a half of acres the rough estimate
of land superficies in Dutch Guiana, about four
hundred thousand acres appear on the public
records as having been, not simultaneously, but
at different times granted out for cultivation,
and of these again not quite thirty thousand are
actually occupied. So that the cultivated land
stands in proportion to that granted as about one-
thirteenth; to the total, of one-fiftieth only. Of

this small oasis amid an ocean of forest, hardly an acre but is situated in the close neighbourhood of the capital, or along the lower courses of the rivers; not a single estate is to be found at a distance of more than forty miles in a straight line from the sea. So much for the east and centre districts. As for Coronie, to the west of the Coppename river, and Nikerie, alongside of the English frontier, they are settlements of recent date, and even more thinly peopled than the rest.

Up the rivers, along the canals, following the bridle-paths, you look around to see what two centuries of Dutch government, of Dutch energy, of Dutch perseverance, have accomplished in a land favoured by nature as are few lands in the New World or the Old. Does the result correspond? Near the capital, indeed, and the harbour, and in the immediate vicinity of the great river-trunks the sight is fair enough; but further up, how unsatisfactory! Estates there certainly are, but how small, how thinly scattered!—rare islets in a trackless ocean of unreclaimed bush, marginal lines by the winding river-courses, desultory fringes to a boundless expanse of wilderness behind. The narrow European domain

includes scarce one-tenth of what the map-maker
assigns to the Batavian colours, and of that tenth
again it is much if one-fifth be under actual cultivation.

Now pass beyond, and explore the practically
non-European nine-tenths of outside territory.
There, amid lofty trees and wide savannas, now
wholly lonely, or only visited by some stray Bush
negro or listless Indian, may yet be seen, we are
told, the ruins of spacious and well-constructed
dwellings, the blurred outlines of once-flourish-
ing estates, the broken and desecrated tombs of
bygone proprietors, the traces of soldierless forts,
choked-up canals, and long-perished labour and
wealth. Thus for the uplands it is "Ichabod"
complete,—they are deserted, dead; for the coast
not so bad, but that too is only half alive,—something there is, but the very goodness of that
something saddens, because there is so little
of it: why is it not more? And if neither the
governors nor the governed, neither the Europeans
nor the creoles, neither the whites nor the
blacks, neither the climate nor the soil, be in
fault,—and in matter of fact none of them are
so,—who then is to blame?

Strictly speaking, no one. But what if the colony has never had a fair chance?—if, from her first starting till now, she has been, without intermission, too heavily handicapped to allow her even a chance of coming forward in the race? And such precisely has been her lot. Her foul days have been out of all proportion to her fair; her difficulties, from without and from within, greater than her means of surmounting them: that they have stunted her is no wonder; the wonder is that they have not put an end to her altogether.

The retrospect is a strange one. In the early days of the " plantation," as it was then called, the high grounds of the interior were cultivated in preference to the coast, because possessed of a healthier climate and a richer soil. Here were Marshall's first tobacco-fields; here Willoughby's indigo growth; here the great sugar estates of Nassy and his Hebrew followers : fair beginnings of speedy prosperity, as speedily blighted. Before the "savannah" had waved with its tenth harvest, began the French hostilities of 1696, that culminated fourteen years later in the sack of Paramaribo, not merely exhausting the actual resources of the

colony, but loading it with heavy debt, and the
still more intolerable burden of a fifty years' servile
war, of which Cassard's invasion was, by the
prostration it left behind, the direct cause and
prelude. Then insurrection followed on insurrection, raid on raid; estate after estate was ravaged;
night by night the sky was reddened by the flames
of burning plantations, and the earth with the
blood of the planters, till the entire inland lay
desolate, and whatever energy remained to the
colonists was perforce driven to take refuge in
the narrow strip of comparative security along
the coast.

With a new field before it, industry took a
fresh start, and at the beginning of the present
century 640 estates along the banks of the Lower
Surinam river and its kindred streams made some
amends for the losses inland. But the evil genius
of the colony lost no time in again interposing
with a series of adversities, less tragic indeed in
kind than the past, but not a whit less injurious
—financial embarrassments, commercial rivalries,
social changes. There is no need to reiterate the
list: I have read it out, at least the principal
headings, before. By 1850 the number of culti-

tivated estates had fallen to 260; in 1862 there
were only 229. Matters were now at their worst,
and accordingly the turn came. Already in
1867 the estates had risen again to 276; five
years later, to 292; at the present date they
exceed 300. May they continue to increase and
multiply till they fill and replenish the land!
there is room and to spare. But this cannot be till
the two great wants, the prime requisites of Surinam as of every other colony, are supplied—
capital and population.

Of the first deficiency, that of capital, and its
causes, I have spoken already. But one main
cause is ignorance. Let Surinam be better
known, she will be better provided; let her name
but become familiar on the European money-
market, and the treasures of that market will find
their way to her before long,—they could take
no better direction, flow into no securer or more
remunerative channels.

Remains last in mention, first in importance,
population. This is to a colony what action is,
if we credit Demosthenes, to an orator; boldness,
in Bacon's estimate, to a statesman; patronage,
as Blake avers, to a painter, and perhaps to others.

And, so that a colony may flourish, be wealthy,
prosperous, successful, what first ? Population. What second ? Population. What
third, thirtieth, three-hundredth if you will?
Population. But let not the word be mis-
construed. By "population" I do not mean
the "sufficient" merely; that is, a population
just adequate to the working of large estates,
with nothing over—enough for a monopoly of
labour and strength, whatever its direction; this
is not the "population" I mean. Or rather it is
this, and something more; this, and a surplus
population into the bargain,—"over-population"
in fact, with an ample margin, after the
large properties of the land have drawn from it
their necessary labour-supply, to create, enclose,
and cultivate those small freeholds, that varied
minor produce, without which staple products
are only an unbuttressed wall; vast exports, a
vast risk; and giant estates, a giant instability.
No cup is truly full till it runs over; no man rich
till he has not enough only, but to spare; no
territory flourishing till it has an over-supply of
labour and life, sufficient not for great uses only,
but for small—for waste at times. And did the

tutelary goddess of Surinam yet enjoy her old
pagan advantages, now lost, alas! to her as to
her fellow-goddesses, of a being and a voice,
"More life and fuller,—*that* I want," would be
her answer to the votaries come to inquire of her
courts.

"Granted; and to this very end we have
within the last three years imported 5,000
coolies," those votaries may reply. So far, so
good. But when we recall to memory the
400,000 acres portioned out to cultivation, and
only tilled to the extent of 30,000, not to
mention the unassigned 1,100,000 acres beyond,
the Adamless Eden of the south, we cannot but
be reminded of certain five small fishes, not of
pagan but Christian tradition, set before a
Syrian crowd of 5,000 and more, and exclaim,
as some one is said to have then not unnaturally
exclaimed, "What are these among so many?"
Nor can a miraculous multiplication be hoped for
to solve the difficulty nowadays. Bear in mind,
too, that of all proposed means for filling up the
popular void, coolie immigration is the most
costly: the initial outlay alone required for each
imported Hindoo—an outlay apart from frequent

extra charges, losses by sickness or death, and all the "sundries" that figure so largely at the foot of every general account—equals or exceeds 34*l.* per head. A Chinese is more expensive still—a serious preliminary absorption of future profits. Prepayments of this kind may be borne once in a way by Dutch Guiana, perhaps twice; but should they have to be often repeated, where, in the name of all the discoverers of unknown quantities, are the funds to come from? The same non-influx of capital that keeps at low ebb, as I have formerly remarked, the vitality of the town, has an even more lowering effect, it is easy to understand, on the vitality of the country. What might happen if the funds were attainable, if Trollope's "million of coolies" loomed as distinct on the Surinam as on the Demerara horizon, I cannot say: millions of hogsheads possibly, and a golden age. But the golden spell for calling them forth from the Indian deep is not written in the estate-books of Dutch Guiana, nor is likely soon to be; certainly not on the "million" scale.

Coolies and Chinese do not, then, form the staff on which Surinam must lean before she can rise.

But European immigration? Tried over and over again, it has failed here neither more completely nor less than elsewhere within the West Indian zone, and for the same reasons. It must always fail. Not because the climate is unhealthy, but because it is unsuited; and experience on this point has been bought so often and so dear, that it is to be hoped no further bands of immigrant European labourers, Dutch, Irish, Scotch, German, or other, will be tempted into buying it again.

But, say some, there is hope of mines to be discovered among the mountain ranges in the far south of the Guiana territory; and on mines what may not follow? Little good, I fear. Long since the world-wide wisdom of "large-browed Verulam" pronounced the sentence, ratified by as world-wide experience, that "the hope of mines is very uncertaine, and useth to make the planters," *i.e.* colonists, "lazie in other things." Mineral treasures are the veriest Pandora-gifts of nature to a land, and that Surinam may be spared the deadly present is the best wish her friends can make in her behalf. Happily, there is not much cause for fearing the contrary. But should ever the ill genius of South America, the "demon

s

of the mine," set up his yellow throne on the banks of her rivers, should the gold, of which particles, fortunately very small ones, washed down stream have from time to time half awakened the dormant cupidity of discoverers, become to Dutch Guiana what it has been to California or Natal, then, indeed, farewell to estates, to agriculture, to honest industry, to true prosperity, to contentment, to hope itself, in Surinam. All will disappear in the devouring mine-gulf; all melt away, fused down into one common mass of rascality and gold. The territory is too narrow to contain at once two masters, the mine and the field; one or other must speedily give way; and the glittering though delusive vistas opened by the former would inevitably efface the sober and substantial prospects offered by the latter from the landscape. The first man who brings in the news of remunerative gold-fields in Upper Surinam ought to have from the colony a rope for his reward; and if it silences his voice before he has time to make his discovery public, so much the better.

The true product-mines of Surinam are her plantations; they lie above ground, not under.

And her most reliable labour-mine is, as in one way or other it always has been, Africa; and, above all, the eastern coasts of that continent, after the manner I have indicated in a previous chapter. The project has, I allow, its difficulties; it might, probably would, meet with opposition all the more serious because based on well-intentioned error; but its advantages are more than its difficulties, and, to sum up all in one, it is, under existing circumstances, the only practical course for obtaining, not merely an immediate and transitory, but a permanent supply of labour and life. Nor is there, I repeat it, anything to fear for the colony or the colonists from a negro immigration, however numerous, under the combined discipline of Dutch rule and Moravian teachership, that has trained the African native into the Surinam creole, the cannibals of Gaboon into the peasants of Munnickendam; there is everything to hope. May the vision become reality!—

Good wishes have been exchanged, hospitalities acknowledged, their renewal offered, hopes of future meetings expressed—all that makes parting bitter sweet; and now the "stelling" is left; and town and tower lessen and disappear behind the nearer river-margin of plantation and tree. We have passed Fort Amsterdam; the river's mouth opens wide on the Atlantic before us! Our little coasting-steamer—she is commanded by the same cheery, semi-Indian captain who last week had our river-craft in charge—will in a day more cast anchor by the Demeraran shore, off the busy wharfs of Georgetown; and Surinam will for me take its place, a thing of the past, in the picture-gallery of other memories of other lands. Nor will it be the least pleasing in the series, nor the least often recalled to view. And, to borrow for Dutch Guiana the words of the same author and the very same chapter cited when I began, " I cannot end this crude epitome of crude views respecting the colony, without saying that I have never met a pleasanter set of people than I found there, or ever passed my hours much more joyously."

INDEX.

THE END.

E. J. FRANCIS AND CO., TOOK'S COURT AND WINE OFFICE COURT, E.C.

For EU product safety concerns, contact us at Calle de José Abascal, 56–1°, 28003 Madrid, Spain or eugpsr@cambridge.org.

 www.ingramcontent.com/pod-product-compliance
Ingram Content Group UK Ltd.
Pitfield, Milton Keynes, MK11 3LW, UK
UKHW010345140625
459647UK00010B/843